VEGETARIAN
COOKING TODAY

Text by Lalita Ahmed, Judith Ferguson,
    Anne Ager and Maureen McCall
Photography by Peter Barry
Designed by Philip Clucas
Produced by Ted Smart and David Gibbon

CLB 1738
This edition published 1986 by Bramley Books, Godalming, Surrey.
© 1986 Illustrations and text: Colour Library Books Ltd.,
    Guildford, Surrey.
Filmsetting by Acesetters Ltd., Richmond, Surrey.
Printed and bound in Barcelona, Spain by Croniòn, S.A.
ISBN 0 86283 489 9
Dep. Leg. B-29.707-86

VEGETARIAN COOKING TODAY

BRAMLEY BOOKS

Introduction

It is amazing how rigid we are when it comes to the subject of food and what we eat. In all other aspects of life virtually anything goes: people walk the streets with pink hair; sail the Atlantic single-handed or jog around the houses for two hours every morning and yet if we prefer beans and lentils to beef and chicken we are considered as being rather odd.

Vegetarians are not cranks, and there is nothing weird and wonderful about a pattern of vegetarian eating; they just prefer to eat dishes which do not contain meat, poultry, game and, quite often, fish. 'Why don't they become ill?' you hear people say; 'Where do they get their energy from if they don't eat meat?'; 'How boring to live on just vegetables and those little dried peas!' As vegetarians will happily tell you, they feel perfectly healthy, have quite sufficient energy to cope with day-to-day activities and, above all, *they really enjoy their food.*

A vegetarian diet can be just as varied and interesting as one based on meat and fish. Meat is much the same the world over, which cannot be said of the wide and wonderful range of fresh fruits and vegetables. And it is variety which is very much the keynote of vegetarian eating: different pastas, rices, cheeses, nuts and pulses are just a selection of the varied ingredients of a vegetarian diet. Most important of all, vegetarian dishes are every bit as nutritious as their meat-rich counterparts. The main difference lies with the types of food which provide us with the necessary nutrients. In a typical vegetarian dish, the protein usually comes from pulses, nuts or cheese, or a combination of these ingredients. Minerals, vitamins, fats and carbohydrates come from all the other basic foods, such as those already mentioned.

Eating 'the vegetarian way' has all sorts of advantages in its favour. A meatless diet is a very healthy one since it is nutritious, low in fat and high in bulk and fibre. Vegetarians rarely need to watch their weight as a diet that is high in natural fibre and low in fat is comparatively low in calories. The traditional pattern of Western eating is relatively expensive to follow, whereas vegetarian dishes are more economical to prepare and cook. In fact, meatless meals can simply make a nice change from the traditional pattern of eating. Vegetarian cooking is fun, and eating vegetarian meals is healthy and good for you.

Vegetarian food really can be exciting and delicious and even if you are not a committed vegetarian many of the ideas in this book are well worth trying. The dishes combine unusual tastes and textures with an imaginative use of spices and fresh herbs for extra flavour. If you served many of the recipes to your family and friends they probably wouldn't even realise that their meal was meatless.

CONTENTS

Chapter One

SOUPS AND APPETISERS

Tomato Saar

This is a thin tomato soup from the South of India. It makes a refreshing and interesting starter.

PREPARATION TIME: 15 minutes
COOKING TIME: 17-18 minutes
SERVES: 4-6 people

10ml (2 tsp) butter
1 small onion, peeled and chopped
225g (½lb) tomatoes, skinned and chopped
1 litre (1¾ pints) water
15ml (1 tblsp) tomato puree
4-6 green curry leaves
Salt and freshly ground black pepper to taste
3 cloves of garlic, peeled and crushed

Garnish
1-2 sprigs fresh green coriander or parsley leaves, chopped
1 green chilli, chopped (optional)

Melt half of the butter and fry the onion for 3-4 minutes. Add the skinned and chopped tomatoes and cook for 5 minutes. Blend the water and tomato puree and add to the onion and tomatoes. Add curry leaves. Season with salt and pepper. Cover and simmer for 5-7 minutes. Heat the remaining butter and fry the crushed cloves of garlic until dark brown. Pour the mixture over the simmering tomato soup. Remove from the heat. Sprinkle over the chopped coriander and chilli. Discard green chilli before eating. Serve piping hot either with French bread or with a little plain boiled rice. Alternatively: blend the skinned tomatoes to give a smooth textured soup.

Daal Soup

This is a thick and hearty soup, made from lentils. The lentils most often used for making soup are red lentils, or yellow lentils which are called Toor daal. The recipe below can be made with either variety.

PREPARATION TIME: 15-20 minutes
COOKING TIME: 15 minutes
SERVES: 4-6 people

350g (12oz) red lentils (see above)
900ml (1½ pints) water
4 canned tomatoes, drained and crushed
1 green chilli, sliced lengthways and seeded
30ml (2 tblsp) natural yogurt or soured cream
15g (½oz) butter
1 medium onion, peeled and chopped
salt and freshly ground black pepper to taste
1-2 sprigs fresh green coriander leaves, chopped

Facing page: Tomato Saar (top right), Daal Soup (top left) and Mixed Vegetable Soup (bottom).

Wash the lentils in 4-5 changes of water. Drain the lentils and put them into a pan with the water. Cover the pan and bring to the boil; simmer for 10 minutes. Beat until smooth with an egg whisk. Add the crushed tomatoes and green chilli and simmer gently for 2 minutes. Stir in the yogurt or soured cream. Melt the butter in a small pan and fry the onion until golden. Season the hot soup with salt and pepper and pour into a serving bowl; sprinkle with the fried onion and chopped coriander. Serve immediately with buttered brown bread, crisp rolls or croutons.

Mixed Vegetable Soup

This Indian recipe can include a wide variety of vegetables. One creates one's own dish by adding or subtracting one or more vegetables.

PREPARATION TIME: 15 minutes

COOKING TIME: about 20 minutes

SERVES: 6 people

10ml (2 tsp) butter
1 medium onion, peeled and chopped
6 cloves
2.5cm (1 inch) piece cinnamon stick
4 small green cardamoms
1 small bayleaf
1 medium potato, peeled and chopped
2 carrots, peeled and chopped
1 banana, peeled and chopped
6 florets of cauliflower
50g (2oz) shelled fresh or frozen peas
1 leek, washed and chopped
1 stick celery, chopped
50g (2oz) green beans (sliced or chopped)
1 litre (1¾ pints) water
Salt and freshly ground black pepper to taste

Garnish
1-2 sprigs fresh green coriander
1-2 green chillies chopped

Melt the butter in a large saucepan and fry the onion for 3 minutes. Add the cloves, cinnamon, cardamom, bayleaf and fry for 1 minute. Add the potato, carrots, banana and cauliflower. Fry for 3 minutes. Add the remaining vegetables and cook for 2-3 minutes. Add water and salt and pepper to taste. Cover and simmer gently for 8-13 minutes until vegetables are cooked. Adjust seasoning. Garnish with chopped coriander leaves and green chillies. Discard green chillies before eating. The vegetables should float in the clear soup; do not blend.

Eggs baked in Tarragon Cream

PREPARATION TIME: 5 minutes

COOKING TIME: 8 minutes

OVEN TEMPERATURE: 180°C, 350°F, Gas Mark 4

SERVES: 4 people

4 large eggs
Nut of butter
60ml (4 tbsps) cream
1 tbsp chopped tarragon
Salt
Pepper

Butter individual oven-proof ramekin dishes. Break an egg into each dish. Add chopped tarragon, and salt and pepper to cream and mix well. Add 15ml (1 tbsp) of cream mixture to each ramekin. Place ramekins on a baking sheet in a pre-heated oven until set, about 6-8 minutes. Serve hot.

Egg Flower

PREPARATION TIME: 20 minutes

COOKING TIME: 15 minutes

SERVES: 4 people

6 eggs
15ml (1 tbsp) vinegar
3 tbsps mayonnaise
15ml (1 tbsp) single cream
5ml (1 tsp) lemon juice (or to taste)
Salt
White pepper

Garnish
Watercress
Pinch of paprika

Fill a saucepan with water and 15ml (1 tbsp) of vinegar and bring to the boil. Reduce heat and simmer. Gently add eggs and cook for 12 minutes. Rinse under cold water to stop cooking. Crack and peel off shells and set eggs aside in a bowl of cold water. Mix together mayonnaise, cream, lemon juice and salt and white pepper to taste. Cut 4 eggs in half. Place yolk-side down in a circle on a serving dish. Cut remaining eggs in half and separate yolks from whites. Rinse whites and cut into shreds. Push yolks through a sieve and set aside. Pour mayonnaise over eggs on serving dish. Sprinkle egg white around outside. Sprinkle yolk on top towards the centre. Sprinkle with paprika. Finally garnish with a bunch of watercress in the centre.

Carrot Soup

PREPARATION TIME: 12 minutes

COOKING TIME: 20-25 minutes

SERVES: 4 people

4-6 carrots, peeled and cut into thick slices
1 medium onion, peeled and quartered
1 medium turnip, peeled and cut into wedges
2 cloves garlic, peeled
750ml (1¼ pints) water or chicken stock
2.5ml (½ tsp) dried thyme
Salt and ground white pepper to taste
Hot pepper sauce to taste

Garnish
25g (1oz) toasted sunflower seeds, flaked almonds and pistachio nuts (mixed together)

Put the carrots, onion, turnip, garlic and water into a large saucepan. Cover and simmer for 15 minutes. Add thyme and salt and pepper to taste and simmer for a further 5 minutes. Cool slightly and blend in a liquidiser. Return to the saucepan and heat the soup through. Ladle the soup into bowls. Add hot pepper sauce to taste. Serve garnished with toasted nuts.

Eggs baked in Tarragon
Cream (left) and Egg Flower
(below).

Gazpacho

PREPARATION TIME:
20 minutes, plus chilling time

SERVES: 4 people

450g (1lb) ripe tomatoes, skinned
  and roughly chopped
1 onion, peeled and diced
1 green pepper, cored, seeds removed,
  and diced

**This page: Tomato and
Pepper Frostie. Facing page:
Gazpacho.**

Half a cucumber
2 tbsps stale white breadcrumbs
2 cloves garlic, crushed
30ml (2 tbsps) red wine vinegar
1 large can tomato juice
Salt
Pepper

Accompaniments
*Diced cucumber, onion, tomato and
green pepper*

Soak breadcrumbs in vinegar. Reserve tomato flesh, and half the onion and half the green pepper for garnish. Blend remaining onion and remaining green pepper with tomato juice, breadcrumbs, vinegar, and garlic, and season to taste.

Push through a sieve. Chill well. Meanwhile, skin and chop cucumber. Serve with crushed ice and small bowls of cucumber, onion, tomato and green pepper.

Onion-Egg-Tomato Bake

PREPARATION TIME:	15 minutes
COOKING TIME:	20 minutes
OVEN TEMPERATURE: 200°C, 400°F, Gas Mark 6	
SERVES:	4 people

4 eggs, hard boiled
2 medium onions, peeled and sliced
60g (2oz) butter or margarine
30g (1oz) flour
150ml (¼ pint) milk
2 tomatoes, skinned and sliced thinly
1 tbsp breadcrumbs
1 tbsp freshly grated Parmesan cheese
Salt
Pepper

Garnish
Parsley

Melt butter in pan. Add onions and fry over gentle heat until softened but not coloured. Remove with a slotted spoon and set aside. Stir in flour and cook for 1 minute. Remove from heat and gradually stir in milk. Beat well and return to heat. Cook for 3 minutes, stirring continuously. Add onions and plenty of seasoning to counteract the sweetness of the onions. Cut eggs in half. Remove yolks, sieve and set aside. Rinse and slice egg whites. Place in the bottom of an ovenproof dish. Cover with onion mixture, then with a layer of sliced tomatoes. Mix together egg yolk, breadcrumbs and Parmesan cheese. Sprinkle over top and place in a hot oven until golden on top. Garnish with parsley.

Celery and Hazelnut Soup

PREPARATION TIME:	15 minutes
COOKING TIME:	30-35 minutes
SERVES:	4 people

1 medium onion, thinly sliced
30ml (2 tblsp) olive oil
6-8 stems celery, finely chopped
1 bayleaf

Celery and Hazelnut Soup (below left), Broccoli Timbales (below right) and Onion-Egg-Tomato Bake (above right).

Salt and freshly ground black pepper
to taste
30ml (2 tblsp) ground hazelnuts
300ml (½ pint) skimmed milk
450ml (¾pint) vegetable stock

Garnish
Small celery leaves
A few flaked hazelnuts

Fry the onion gently in the olive oil for 3 minutes. Add the celery and fry for a further 3 minutes. Add the bayleaf, salt and pepper to taste, ground hazelnuts, skimmed milk and stock. Bring to the boil and simmer gently for 20-25 minutes. Blend the soup in the liquidiser until smooth. Reheat the soup gently in a clean saucepan. Serve each portion garnished with a celery leaf and a sprinkling of flaked hazelnuts.

Broccoli Timbales

PREPARATION TIME:	10 minutes
COOKING TIME:	30 minutes
OVEN TEMPERATURE: 190°C, 375°F, Gas Mark 5	
SERVES:	4 people

4 broccoli florets
30g (1oz) butter or margarine
30g (1oz) plain flour
300ml (½ pint) milk
1 tsp ground nutmeg
2 eggs, beaten
Salt
Pepper

Blanch broccoli in boiling salted water for 3 minutes. Drain and refresh under cold water. Drain and set aside. Melt butter in pan. Stir in flour and nutmeg and cook for 1 minute. Remove from heat and stir in milk gradually. Return to heat and bring to the boil, stirring continuously. Cook for 3 minutes. Add salt and white pepper to taste and beat well. Set aside to cool. Butter 4 ramekin dishes. Place a floret of broccoli in each dish with stem pointing upwards. Beat eggs into cooled white sauce, and pour into each ramekin dish. Place

ramekins in a shallow baking tin. Pour boiling water into tin to a depth of 2.5cm (1"). Bake in a pre-heated oven for 15 minutes, or until just setting. Remove from oven and turn out onto individual plates. Serve immediately.

Tomato and Pepper Frostie

PREPARATION TIME: 15 minutes, plus freezing time	
SERVES: 4 people	

¼ cup tomato juice
Juice of 1 lemon
6 ice cubes
5ml (1 tsp) soy sauce
½ small green pepper
½ small red pepper
Garnish
4 tomato flowers

Crush ice. Put tomato juice, lemon juice, ice and soy sauce in blender. Blend together. Put into ice-trays and place in freezer for ½ hour or until half-frozen. Meanwhile, remove core and seeds from peppers and dice finely. Remove tomato ice from freezer and transfer to a bowl, breaking up with the back of a fork. Mix in peppers. Re-freeze for a further 2 hours, stirring occasionally. For a garnish, make tomato flowers. Peel tomatoes (drop into boiling water; count to ten slowly; then rinse in cold water; remove skins). Starting at one end, with a sharp knife slice a continuous strip around the tomato. Form into a rose shape. Serve on top of tomato and pepper frostie.

Rice and Mushroom Soup

Ideal for a party or for summer afternoons.

PREPARATION TIME:	10 minutes
COOKING TIME:	40-50 minutes
SERVES:	6-8 people

125g (4oz) wild rice or brown rice
250ml (8 fl oz) water
25g (1oz) butter
1 medium onion, peeled and finely chopped
1 stem celery, chopped
100g (4oz) mushrooms, chopped
2.5ml (½ tsp) powdered garam masala
2.5ml (½ tsp) ground mustard seed
Salt and freshly ground black pepper to taste
1 litre (1¾ pints) water or stock
22ml (1½ tblsp) cornflour blended with
30ml (2 tblsp) water
75ml (5 tblsp) single cream

Garnish
1-2 sprigs fresh green coriander or parsley, chopped

Wash the rice in 3-4 changes of water; cook covered in 250ml (8 fl oz) water for 25-30 minutes, or until rice is tender. Keep on one side. Melt the butter in a large saucepan; saute the onion until tender for 3-5 minutes. Add the celery and mushrooms. Cook for 1-2 minutes. Stir in the powdered garam masala, mustard and salt and pepper to taste. Add the water or stock. Simmer for 5 minutes. Add the cornflour mixture and simmer for a further 3 minutes. Add the cooked rice and cream. Gently stir over a low heat for 2 minutes to heat through. Ladle the soup into bowls and garnish with coriander or parsley.

Cucumber Soup

PREPARATION TIME:	15 minutes
COOKING TIME:	8-10 minutes
SERVES:	4 people

1 large cucumber
250ml (8 fl oz) water
600ml (1 pint) vegetable stock
15ml (1 tblsp) white wine vinegar
30ml (2 tblsp) cornflour mixed with
30ml (2 tblsp) water
30ml (2 tblsp) soured cream
30ml (2 tblsp) natural yogurt
Salt and ground white pepper to taste

15ml (1 tblsp) chopped chives or
  green spring onion tops
Chilli powder

Cut ¼ of the cucumber into wafer
thin rounds and keep aside for

garnishing. Puree the rest of the
cucumber with the water in a
liquidiser. Put the vegetable stock
and the pureed cucumber into a
saucepan and bring to the boil over
a medium heat. Add the vinegar

**This page: Carrot Soup (top),
Rice and Mushroom Soup
(centre) and Cucumber Soup
(bottom).**

and cook for 1 minute. Add the cornflour mixture gradually. Stir well until the soup starts to thicken. Simmer for 2-3 minutes. Remove from the heat and cool slightly. Blend in the liquidiser and add the soured cream and yogurt. Return to the saucepan and season with salt and pepper. Heat through gently to serve hot or chill to serve cold. Serve garnished with sliced cucumber and chopped chives or spring onion tops. Sprinkle with chilli powder.

Pepper Appetiser

| PREPARATION TIME: 15 minutes |
| COOKING TIME: 1 hour 15 minutes |
| SERVES: 4 people |

1 green pepper
1 red pepper
2 tomatoes
2 onions
60ml (4 tbsps) white vinegar
30ml (2 tbsps) oil
Salt

Remove core and seeds from peppers and slice lengthways. Peel and slice onions and tomatoes. Heat oil in a large suacepan. Add vegetables and salt to taste and simmer, covered, for 1 hour, stirring occasionally. Remove lid and add vinegar, and simmer for a further 15 minutes. Allow to cool, and chill in refrigerator.

Onion Soup

Onion soup has been made famous by the French. Here is a delicious recipe based on the French style.

| PREPARATION TIME: 20 minutes |
| COOKING TIME: 1 hour |
| SERVES: 4-6 people |

75g (3oz) butter
3-4 large onions, peeled and sliced into rings
30ml (2 tblsp) flour
900ml (1½ pints) vegetable stock
Salt and ground white pepper to taste
6 slices of French bread 1½cm

Facing page: Melon Balls in
Mulled Wine. Pepper
Appetiser (left) and
Aubergine Appetiser
(below).

(¾ inch) thick
2 cloves of garlic, peeled and bruised
75g (3oz) grated Parmesan cheese

Melt the butter in a saucepan and fry the onions briskly on a very low heat. Cover and simmer the onions in their own juices for 25-30 minutes, stirring occasionally until golden brown. Remove from the heat. Stir in the flour and add the stock gradually. Season with salt and pepper and return to heat. Bring to the boil quickly; reduce the heat and simmer covered for 15-20 minutes. Rub the bread pieces each side with the bruised garlic. Float the bread rounds in the soup and sprinkle grated Parmesan cheese generously over the top. Put under the grill and cook for 2-3 minutes or until the top is golden. Serve at once. Alternatively – fry the bread rounds or bread slices in butter prior to rubbing with garlic.

Quick Tomato Soup (above right), Minestrone Soup (right) and Onion Soup (far right).

Minestrone Soup

This famous vegetable and pasta soup from Italy can be made in many different ways. The recipe below is a simple, but delicious one – served with bread, it is a complete meal in itself.

PREPARATION TIME: 20 minutes
COOKING TIME: 30 minutes
SERVES: 4-6 people

45ml (3 tblsp) olive oil
1 medium onion, peeled and chopped
2 cloves of garlic, peeled and crushed
2 medium potatoes, peeled and diced
3 carrots, peeled and diced
2 stems celery, chopped
175g (6oz) shredded cabbage
4-5 skinned or canned tomatoes, chopped
900ml (1½ pints) water or vegetable stock
1 bouquet garni
175g (6oz) shelled fresh, or frozen peas
50g (2oz) boiled and cooked red kidney beans
100g (4oz) macaroni or any shaped pasta
Salt and freshly ground black pepper to taste
50g (2oz) grated Parmesan cheese

Heat the olive oil in a saucepan and fry the onion and garlic until the onion is soft, 2-3 minutes. Stir in the potatoes, carrots and celery and fry for 3 minutes; add the cabbage and tomatoes. Cook for 5-6 minutes. Add water or stock and bouquet garni. Add peas, kidney beans, pasta and simmer gently, covered, for 10-15 minutes, or until the pasta is just tender. Season with salt and pepper and ladle into bowls. Sprinkle generously with grated Parmesan cheese before serving. Serve Minestrone soup with crusty bread.

Quick Tomato Soup

This is quite an exotic soup and is made within a few minutes. It is ideal for a hot summer's day.

PREPARATION TIME: 10 minutes plus chilling time

SERVES: 4-6 people

600ml (1 pint) chilled tomato juice
50g (2oz) fresh or canned tomato
    puree, chilled
2.5ml (½ tsp) hot red pepper sauce
2.5ml (½ tsp) grated lemon peel
2.5ml (½ tsp) grated orange peel
45-60ml (3-4 tblsp) dry white wine
Salt and ground white pepper to taste
Little iced water
45ml (3 tblsp) natural yogurt
60ml (4 tblsp) soured cream
6 balls of honeydew melon
6 balls of water melon
6 balls of ripe pear

Garnish
Mint leaves

Mix the tomato juice, tomato puree, pepper sauce, fruit peels and wine together. Season with salt and pepper, cover and refrigerate for 3-4 hours. Thin the soup with a little iced water if necessary. Whisk the yogurt and cream together until smooth and light. Divide the soup amongst 4-6 bowls. Spoon the yogurt and cream mixture into the centre of each portion and float the fruit balls on top. Garnish with mint leaves and serve.

Aubergine Appetiser

PREPARATION TIME: 15 minutes

COOKING TIME: 20 minutes

SERVES: 4 people

1 large aubergine
2 ripe tomatoes, peeled, seeds
    removed, and chopped
2 cloves garlic, crushed
60ml (4 tbsps) oil
1 tbsp tomato purée
60ml (4 tbsps) water
Salt
Pepper

Cut aubergine lengthwise into strips 1cm x 6cm (¼" x 2½"). Heat oil in pan until hot. Add aubergine and cook for 5 minutes or until cooked. Remove from pan with slotted spoon. Add extra oil as necessary and heat. Fry garlic for 30 seconds. Add tomatoes, tomato purée, salt and pepper, and water and cook for 10 minutes or until sauce is thick. Add aubergine and stir together. Adjust seasoning and cook for a further 5 minutes. Serve hot or cold.

Melon Balls in Mulled Wine

PREPARATION TIME: 1 hour

COOKING TIME: 10 minutes

SERVES: 4 people

1 melon
½ bottle red wine
2 cinnamon sticks
4 cloves
3 blades mace
Juice and pared rind of 1 orange
1 tsp freshly grated nutmeg
60g (2oz) granulated sugar

Put wine, orange juice and rind, spices and sugar into a pan and heat gently. Do not allow to boil. When hot, remove from heat and leave to infuse for an hour. Strain. Meanwhile, cut melon in half and scrape out pips. Then make melon balls with a melon-ball scoop, or cut into chunks. Place in individual serving dishes and pour over mulled wine.

Avocado Lemon Ring

PREPARATION TIME:
10 minutes, plus setting time

SERVES: 4 people

2 avocado pears
1 pkt lemon jelly
150ml (¼ pint) hot water
1 lemon
10ml (2 tsp) soy sauce
150ml (¼ pint) double cream
Salt

Garnish
Slices of lemon
Watercress

Dissolve the jelly in hot water and leave to cool. Grate finely the rind of the lemon, and squeeze and strain the juice. Peel the avocado pears and remove the pips. Mash well with a fork. Pour on the cooled jelly and whisk or blend. Add lemon juice, rind, soy sauce, a pinch of salt and cream, and mix well. Pour into dampened ring mould and leave to set. Turn out to serve and garnish with slices of lemon and watercress in centre.

Grilled Grapefruit

PREPARATION TIME: 45 minutes

COOKING TIME: 10 minutes

SERVES: 4 people

2 grapefruit
60g (2oz) brown sugar
30ml (2 tbsps) Grand Marnier or
    Cointreau liqueur
1 tbsp clear honey

Garnish
Fresh or maraschino cherries
Fresh mint leaf

Cut grapefruit in half around equators. With a grapefruit knife or sharp knife, cut around edge between flesh of fruit and pith. Then cut down between each segment, removing skin from flesh. Take core between finger and thumb and pull out, removing with skin. Remove any pips. Pour excess juice into bowl. Sprinkle each grapefruit half with sugar and pour over liqueur. Leave to stand for 30 minutes. Meanwhile, mix together honey and grapefruit juice. Pre-heat grill. Pour over honey/grapefruit juice mixture and grill until just browning on top. Trim away any burnt skin and garnish with a cherry and mint leaf.

Facing page: Grilled Grapefruit (top) and Avocado Lemon Ring (bottom).

Chapter Two
SALADS AND SIDE DISHES

Stir-Fried Vegetable Medley

PREPARATION TIME: 20 minutes
COOKING TIME: 10 minutes
SERVES: 4 people as a vegetable

2 carrots, cut into flowers (slice strips
    out lengthways to produce flowers
    when cut across into rounds)
1 can baby sweetcorn, drained
2 cups broccoli florets (slit stems to
    ensure quick cooking)
1 onion, peeled and sliced in julienne
    strips
2 sticks celery, with tough strings
    removed, sliced diagonally in half-
    moon shapes
1 courgette, sliced diagonally
1 clove garlic, crushed
15ml (1 tbsp) light soy sauce
¼ tsp finely-grated ginger
30ml (2 tbsps) oil
Salt
Pepper

Prepare all ingredients before
starting to cook. Heat wok and add
oil. Add ginger, garlic, onion,
carrots, broccoli and courgette, and
toss in oil for 2-3 minutes. Add
celery and baby sweetcorn, and toss
1-2 minutes longer. Season with
soy sauce, and salt and pepper if
desired. Add cornflour to thicken
vegetable juices if necessary.

Sweet and Sour Cabbage

PREPARATION TIME: 5 minutes
COOKING TIME: 20 minutes
SERVES: 4 people as a vegetable

Half a small cabbage
30g (1oz) butter or margarine
45ml (3 tbsps) vinegar

2 tbsps sugar
45ml (3 tbsps) water
Salt
Pepper

Slice cabbage into shreds. Melt
butter in wok. Put cabbage into
wok with other ingredients and set
over a moderate heat. Stir until hot,
then cover and simmer for
15 minutes. Adjust seasoning if
necessary. Serve hot. Good with
sausages and mashed potato.

Coleslaw

225g (8oz) Dutch cabbage, finely
    shredded
2 radishes, finely sliced
¼ cucumber, finely diced
1 stick celery, finely diced
¼ green pepper, cored, seeded and
    finely sliced
¼ red pepper, cored, seeded and
    finely sliced
1 apple, peeled and finely sliced
1 large carrot, peeled and coarsely
    grated
Mustard and cress or watercress
Salad cream for dressing

Mix the ingredients thoroughly
together in a large bowl and dress
with the salad cream. Garnish with
mustard and cress or watercress.

Bean Salad

175g (6oz) can kidney beans,
    drained
400g (14oz) can sliced green beans,
    drained
1 small onion, peeled and chopped
1 stalk celery, peeled and chopped
45ml (3 tblsp) wine vinegar
15ml (1 tblsp) oil

Few drops of sugar substitute
Salt and pepper

Mix the beans, chopped onion and
chopped celery together. Mix the
vinegar, oil, sugar substitute and
seasoning together. Pour over the
salad and leave to marinate in the
dressing for a few hours, stirring
occasionally. Serve well chilled with
cold, lean meat.

Cucumber and Tomato Salad

450g (1lb) tomatoes, chopped
½ cucumber, finely diced
30ml (2 tblsp) French dressing
Watercress to garnish

Toss the cucumber and tomato in
the French dressing. Garnish with
watercress.

Pineapple, Cheese and Celery Salad

120g (4oz) pineapple pieces
120g (4oz) cheese, diced
¼ head of celery, coarsely sliced
Salad cream for dressing
Lettuce
Watercress to garnish

Drain the pineapple and cut into
small cubes. Toss with the other
ingredients. Serve on a bed of
lettuce, garnished with watercress.

**Facing page: Stir-Fried
Vegetable Medley (top) and
Sweet and Sour Cabbage
(bottom).**

Pasta Salad

100g (4oz) spaghetti
Knob of butter
2 carrots, peeled and coarsely grated
25g (1oz) raisins
6 radishes, finely sliced
¼ green pepper, cored, seeded and
    finely sliced
¼ red pepper, cored, seeded and
    finely sliced

30ml (2 tblsp) French dressing
Watercress or mustard and cress to
    garnish

Boil the spaghetti in salted water
for 10-15 minutes. Drain well, toss
in the butter and leave to cool. Put
all vegetables and raisins together
in a bowl and mix well. Toss in the
French dressing. Garnish with
watercress or mustard and cress.

**This page: Bean Salad
(top), Coleslaw (centre)
and Pasta Salad (bottom).
Facing page: Cucumber
and Tomato Salad (top),
Rice Salad (centre) and
Pineapple, Cheese and
Celery Salad (bottom).**

Butter Beans and Green Capsicum

PREPARATION TIME: 10 minutes
COOKING TIME: 10 minutes

15ml (1 tblsp) oil
1 onion, peeled and chopped
225g (8oz) butter beans or broad
  beans
1 large green pepper, seeded and
  chopped
1.25ml (¼ tsp) turmeric
2.5ml (½ tsp) chilli powder
5ml (1 tsp) ground coriander
Salt to taste
4-5 fresh or canned tomatoes,
  chopped
1 green chilli, chopped
1 sprig fresh coriander leaves,
  chopped

Heat oil and fry onion for 3-4 minutes. Add beans and green pepper. Cook for 4-5 minutes. Sprinkle with turmeric, chilli and ground coriander. Add salt and tomatoes. Mix well. Cover and cook for 5-6 minutes on low heat. Add green chilli and fresh coriander. Cook covered for 2-3 minutes. If too dry add 30ml (2 tblsp) water. This is a dry dish.

Stuffed Peppers

PREPARATION TIME: 20 minutes
COOKING TIME: 30-35 minutes

50g (2oz) ghee or
45ml (3 tblsp) oil
1 onion, peeled and finely chopped
1 potato, peeled and diced
225g (8oz) mixed frozen vegetables
5ml (1 tsp) garam masala powder
2.5ml (½ tsp) chilli powder
10ml (2 tsp) dried mango powder
Salt to taste
6-8 small green peppers
Oil

Heat ghee or oil and fry onion until tender (3-4 minutes). Add potatoes and cook for 4-5 minutes. Add mixed vegetables, and sprinkle with garam masala, chilli powder, mango powder and salt to taste. Cover and cook gently until

This page: Narangi Piyaz Salad (top) and Red Cabbage and Carrot Salad (bottom). Facing page: Butter Beans and Green Capsicum (top), Aloo Gobi (centre) and Stuffed Peppers (bottom).

potatoes are tender. Remove from heat and cool. Wash and wipe dry green peppers. Remove top by slicing across to form a lid. Remove pith and seeds. Heat 45ml (3 tblsp) oil and fry peppers laid sideways, for 1-2 minutes, cooking on all sides. Drain well. Fill each pepper with filling and arrange them on a baking tray and bake in preheated oven, Gas Mark 3 (160°C or 325°F) for 20 minutes. Serve.

Narangi Piyaz Salad (ONION AND ORANGE SALAD)

PREPARATION TIME: 15 minutes

2 large seedless oranges or
4 satsumas
6 spring onions, finely chopped,
  including green leaves
Salt
10ml (2 tsp) lemon juice
1.25ml (¼ tsp) ground black pepper
2.5ml (½ tsp) sugar
10ml (2 tsp) salad oil

Peel oranges and separate into segments. Cut each segment in two. Add onions, salt, lemon juice, pepper, sugar and oil. Gently toss to mix. Serve as a side salad.

Fennel au Gratin

PREPARATION TIME: 15 minutes

COOKING TIME: 25-30 minutes

OVEN: 190°C, 375°F, Gas Mark 5

SERVES: 4 people

4 medium size heads of fennel
Juice of 1 lemon
Salt and freshly ground black pepper
    to taste
25g (1oz) butter
22g (¾oz) flour
150ml (¼ pint) skimmed milk
150ml (¼ pint) dry white wine
60ml (4 tblsp) natural yogurt
2.5ml (½ tsp) chive mustard
75g (3oz) grated Gruyere cheese

Garnish
15ml (1 tblsp) chopped chives

Trim both ends of the fennel –
reserve any feathery tops for
garnish. Peel off any discoloured
patches from the fennel. Cut each
head in half lengthways. Put the
fennel into a pan of boiling water to
which you have added the lemon
juice and 5ml (1 tsp) salt; simmer
steadily for 5 minutes. Drain the
par-cooked fennel thoroughly. Melt
the butter in a pan and stir in the
flour; gradually stir in the milk and
white wine. Bring to the boil and
stir until lightly thickened. Beat in
the yogurt, chive mustard, half the
grated cheese, and salt and pepper
to taste. Arrange the fennel in a
lightly greased ovenproof dish and
spoon the sauce evenly over the
top; sprinkle with the remaining
grated cheese. Bake in the oven for
25-30 minutes, until the sauce is
golden. Garnish with the chopped
chives and any reserved pieces of
feathery fennel.

Mushrooms Monègasque

PREPARATION TIME: 10 minutes,
plus chilling time

COOKING TIME: about 13
                    minutes

SERVES: 4 people

450g (1lb) tomatoes, skinned, seeded
    and chopped
150ml (¼ pint) red wine
30ml (2 tblsp) tomato puree
Pinch ground ginger
Salt and freshly ground black pepper
    to taste
1 clove garlic, peeled and finely
    chopped
2 spring onions, finely chopped
30ml (2 tblsp) raisins
225g (8oz) small button mushrooms

To Serve
Crusty wholemeal bread or rolls

Put the chopped tomatoes, red
wine, tomato puree, ground ginger,
salt and pepper to taste, and the
garlic into a shallow pan. Simmer
for 6-8 minutes. Add the spring
onions, raisins and button
mushrooms; cover the pan and
simmer for 5 minutes. Allow to
cool and then chill very thoroughly.
Serve in small, shallow dishes,
accompanied by crusty wholemeal
bread.

Corn on the Cob

Strip off the husks and remove the
silky threads. Cook the corn on the
cob in boiling water for about 10-
15 minutes, adding a little salt at
the end of the cooking time. When
cooked, drain. Serve with melted
butter.

Braised Celery

25g (1oz) butter
2 medium-sized carrots, peeled and
    diced
8 sticks celery, scrubbed, trimmed
    and cut in half lengthways
300ml (1/2 pint) vegetable stock
Salt and pepper
Chopped parsley to garnish

Heat the butter and fry the carrots
for a few minutes. Add the celery
and cook for a further 2 minutes.
Place the vegetables in an
ovenproof dish and pour on the
stock. Season well. Cover and cook
in the oven for about 1-1¼ hours
at 180°C, 350°F, Gas Mark 4.
Garnish with chopped parsley.

Roast Parsnips

450g (1lb) parsnips, peeled,
    quartered and sliced

Garnish
Chopped fresh parsley

Cook the prepared parsnips in
boiling, salted water for about 5
minutes. Drain well. Place in the fat
around the joint and cook for
about 45 minutes. Garnish with
chopped parsley.

Beetroot (Boiled)

Boil beetroot in a saucepan for 1-
1½ hours. Do not damage the skin
before cooking. The skin will peel
off easily once the beetroot is
cooked.

**Mushrooms Monegasque
(above left) and Fennel au
Gratin (left).**

Red Cabbage and Carrot Salad

PREPARATION TIME: 10 minutes

½ small red cabbage, finely chopped
2-3 carrots, peeled and grated
50g (2oz) raisins
5ml (1 tsp) sugar
1.25ml (¼ tsp) salt or to taste
150ml (¼ pint) soured cream
10ml (2 tsp) lemon juice

Mix cabbage, carrots and raisins. Sprinkle with sugar and salt and pour over the well-stirred soured cream. Sprinkle with lemon juice and mix well. Serve with any meal as a side salad. In place of soured cream, plain salad cream may be used.

Leeks

675g (1½lb) fresh leeks, washed, trimmed and halved
Butter
Pepper

Cook the prepared leeks in boiling, salted water for 10 minutes. Drain and toss in butter and add pepper.

Rice Salad

100g (4oz) patna rice
75g (3oz) pineapple pieces
150g (5oz) sweet corn
2 radishes, finely sliced
¼ red pepper, cored, seeded and finely sliced
¼ green pepper, cored, seeded and finely sliced
French dressing
Watercress or cucumber slices to garnish

Boil the rice in salted water for 15 minutes. Drain well and cool. Drain the pineapple thoroughly and cut into small cubes. Mix all the ingredients together in a bowl and toss in French dressing. Garnish with watercress or slices of cucumber.

Apple and Nut Salad

Salt and pepper
Pinch of dry mustard
45ml (3 tblsp) corn or olive oil
15ml (1 tblsp) wine vinegar
3 red eating apples, peeled and cored
8 sticks of celery, scrubbed and chopped
50g (2oz) chopped peanuts
Chopped fresh parsley to garnish

Put salt, pepper, mustard, oil and vinegar into a screw-topped jar and shake well. Put the apples and celery in a bowl with the chopped nuts. Pour the dressing over the apples and celery and toss well. Spoon into a serving dish and garnish with chopped parsley.

Mushroom Salad

Salt and pepper
Pinch of dry English mustard
135ml (4½ fl oz) oil
45ml (3 tblsp) wine vinegar
15ml (1 tblsp) chopped fresh parsley
1 garlic clove, peeled and crushed
350g (12oz) button mushrooms, sliced

Put the salt, pepper, mustard, oil, vinegar, parsley and garlic into a screw-topped jar and shake well. Pour over the mushrooms in a bowl. Leave to stand for 1 hour then serve.

French Dressing

15g (½oz) sugar
1.25ml (¼ tsp) salt
1.25ml (¼ tsp) dry mustard
150ml (¼ pint) vinegar
300ml (½ pint) corn oil

Blend the sugar, salt and mustard with the vinegar. Gradually beat or whisk in the oil, a little at a time. Taste and adjust the seasoning if necessary. Pour the dressing into a screw-topped jar. Shake vigorously before using, as the oil and vinegar will separate if left to stand.

Aloo Gobi

PREPARATION TIME: 10 minutes
COOKING TIME: 10-12 minutes

1 large onion, peeled and chopped
75g (3oz) ghee or
45ml (3 tblsp) oil
2 medium potatoes, peeled and cut into chunks
1 medium cauliflower, cut into small florets
2-3 green chillis, chopped
2 sprigs fresh coriander leaves, chopped
3.75cm (1½ inch) ginger root, peeled and finely chopped
Salt to taste
Juice of 1 lemon
10ml (2 tsp) garam masala

Fry onion in ghee or oil until just tender, 2-3 minutes. Add potatoes and fry for 2-3 minutes. Add cauliflower and stir fry for 4-5 minutes. Add green chillis, coriander, ginger and salt. Mix well. Cover and cook for 5-6 minutes on low heat, or until potatoes are tender. Sprinkle with lemon juice and garam masala before serving. Serve with parathas.

Kidney Beans and Onion

Salt and pepper
Pinch of dry English mustard
2.5ml (½ tsp) dried basil
1 garlic clove, peeled and crushed
45ml (3 tblsp) olive or corn oil
15ml (1 tblsp) wine vinegar
1 small onion, peeled and sliced
400g (14oz) can of red kidney beans, drained
Chopped parsley to garnish

Facing page: Apple and Nut Salad (top), Kidney Beans and Onion (centre) and Mushroom Salad (bottom).

Combine the salt, pepper, mustard, basil, garlic, oil and vinegar in a screw-topped jar. Lay the onion rings on a plate and sprinkle with salt. Leave for 30 minutes. Drain and rinse in cold water. Place the beans in a bowl, add the onion and toss in the dressing. Garnish with the chopped parsley and serve.

Aloo Methi
(POTATO AND FRESH FENUGREEK LEAVES)

PREPARATION TIME: 10 minutes
COOKING TIME: 10 minutes

50g (2oz) ghee or
45ml (3 tblsp) oil
5ml (1 tsp) cumin seed
1 pinch asafoetida (hing)
3 medium potatoes, peeled and cut into chunks
1 bunch fresh methi leaves, chopped

Aloo Gajjar (above), Toorai Tarkari (right) and Aloo Methi (far right).

5ml (1 tsp) chilli powder
5ml (1 tsp) coriander powder
Salt
1.25ml (¼ tsp) turmeric powder
Juice of 1 lemon

Heat ghee or oil and add cumin seed and hing. When seeds begin to crackle, add potatoes. Fry and cook potatoes for 3-4 minutes then add methi leaves. Mix well and sprinkle with chilli powder, coriander, salt and turmeric powder. Stir the mixture to distribute spices evenly. Cover and cook on low heat for 6-8 minutes. Add lemon juice before serving.

Toorai Tarkari
(COURGETTE CURRY)

PREPARATION TIME: 10 minutes

COOKING TIME: 15 minutes

22ml (1½ tblsp) oil
5ml (1 tsp) cumin seeds
225g (½lb) courgettes, peeled and sliced into quarter inch thick rounds
2.5ml (½ tsp) chilli powder
5ml (1 tsp) ground coriander
1.25ml (¼ tsp) turmeric powder

3-4 fresh or canned tomatoes, chopped
Salt to taste
1 green chilli, halved
1 sprig fresh coriander leaves, chopped

Heat oil and add cumin seeds. When they crackle, add courgette slices. Stir and sprinkle with chilli, coriander and turmeric powder. Mix well and add chopped tomatoes. Sprinkle with salt, green chilli and fresh coriander. Cover and cook for 10-12 minutes.

Green Bean Bhaji

PREPARATION TIME: 10 minutes

COOKING TIME: 10-12 minutes

45ml (3 tblsp) oil or melted ghee
5ml (1 tsp) urid daal
2-3 green chillis
6-8 fresh curry leaves

350g (12oz) frozen sliced green
   beans, unthawed
Salt to taste
15ml (1 tblsp) desiccated coconut

Heat oil or ghee and add urid daal,
green chilli and curry leaves. Stir fry
for half a minute. Add beans and
sprinkle with salt. Cover and cook

**This page: Gado Gado.
Facing page: Green Bean
Bhaji (top), Mili-Juli Sabzi
(bottom right) and
Mushroom Aloo Bhaji
(bottom left).**

for 6-8 minutes. Sprinkle with coconut and mix well. Cover and cook for 3-4 minutes. Serve with chapatis.

Gado Gado

PREPARATION TIME: 20 minutes

COOKING TIME: 30 minutes

SERVES: 4 people as a vegetable

115g (4oz) bean-sprouts
115g (4oz) Chinese cabbage, shredded
115g (4oz) green beans, trimmed
Half a cucumber, cut into batons
1 carrot, peeled and cut into thin strips
1 potato, peeled and cut into thin strips
15ml (1 tbsp) peanut oil

Peanut Sauce
30ml (2 tbsps) peanut oil
60g (2oz) raw shelled peanuts
2 red chillies, seeds removed, and chopped finely, or 1 tsp chilli powder
2 shallots, peeled and chopped finely
1 clove garlic, crushed
1 tsp brown sugar
Juice of half a lemon
100ml (⅙ pint) coconut milk
150ml (¼ pint) water
Salt

Garnish
Sliced hard-boiled eggs
Sliced cucumber

Heat wok and add 15ml (1 tbsp) peanut oil. When hot, toss in carrot and potato. Stir-fry for 2 minutes and add green beans and cabbage. Cook for a further 3 minutes. Add bean-sprouts and cucumber, and stir-fry for 2 minutes. Place in a serving dish.

Make peanut sauce. Heat wok, add 30ml (2 tbsps) peanut oil, and fry peanuts for 2-3 minutes. Remove and drain on absorbent paper. Blend or pound chillies, shallots and garlic to a smooth paste. Grind or blend peanuts to a powder. Heat oil and fry chilli paste for 2 minutes. Add water, and bring to the boil.

Add peanuts, brown sugar, lemon juice, and salt to taste. Stir until sauce is thick – about 10 minutes – and add coconut milk. Garnish vegetable dish with slices of hard-boiled egg, and cucumber and serve with peanut sauce.

Aloo Gajjar
(POTATO AND CARROTS)

PREPARATION TIME: 10 minutes

COOKING TIME: 10-15 minutes

50g (2oz) ghee or
30ml (2 tblsp) oil
5ml (1 tsp) cumin seeds
2 medium potatoes, peeled and cut into 1cm (½ inch) cubes
3 medium carrots, scraped and cubed
5ml (1 tsp) chilli powder
5ml (1 tsp) ground coriander
1.25ml (¼ tsp) turmeric powder
Salt to taste
Juice of half a lemon

Heat ghee or oil and add cumin seeds. When they begin to crackle, add potatoes. Fry for 3-4 minutes then add carrots. Stir the mixture and sprinkle with chilli, coriander, turmeric powder and salt. Stir fry the mixture for 1-2 minutes then cover and cook on low heat for 8-10 minutes. Sprinkle with a little water to help cook carrots. Sprinkle with lemon juice before serving.

Mili-Juli Sabzi
(MIXED VEGETABLE BHAJI)

PREPARATION TIME: 15 minutes

COOKING TIME: 10-15 minutes

50g (2oz) ghee or
45ml (3 tblsp) oil
1 onion, peeled and chopped
5ml (1 tsp) cumin seeds
1 medium potato, peeled and chopped
3 cauliflower florets, cut into small pieces

1 small aubergine, cubed
1 medium green pepper, seeded and cubed
225g (½lb) mixed frozen vegetables
Salt to taste
5ml (1 tsp) turmeric powder
5ml (1 tsp) ground coriander
5ml (1 tsp) chilli powder
3-4 fresh tomatoes, chopped
2 sprigs green fresh coriander leaves, chopped
1-2 green chillis, chopped

Heat ghee or oil and fry onion and cumin seeds for 2-3 minutes. Add potatoes and stir fry for 4-5 minutes. Add cauliflower, aubergine and green pepper and cook for 4 minutes. Add mixed vegetables. Stir to mix well. Sprinkle with salt, turmeric, coriander and chilli powder. Add chopped tomato. Stir and cover. Cook on low heat for 5-6 minutes. Add fresh coriander and chopped chilli. Mix and serve. To make moist curry add 150ml (¼ pint) water after tomatoes are added.

Mushroom Aloo Bhaji
(POTATO AND MUSHROOM BHAJI)

PREPARATION TIME: 5-6 minutes

COOKING TIME: 10-12 minutes

50g (2oz) ghee or
45ml (3 tblsp) oil
1 onion, peeled and chopped
450g (1lb) medium potato, peeled and cubed
2.5ml (½ tsp) salt to taste
30ml (2 tblsp) garam masala powder
225g (½lb) button mushrooms, sliced
Lemon juice

Heat ghee or oil and fry onion until tender (2-3 minutes). Add potatoes and fry for 5-6 minutes. Sprinkle with salt and garam masala. Mix well and cover. Cook for 4-5 minutes until potatoes are tender. Add mushrooms. Stir well. Cover and cook for 2-3 minutes. Sprinkle with lemon juice to taste. Remove from heat and serve.

Chapter Three

PASTA, RICE AND PULSES

Pasta Spirals with Peas and Tomatoes

PREPARATION TIME: 5 minutes

COOKING TIME: 15 minutes

300g (10oz) pasta spirals
350g (12oz) peas

1 tsp sugar
400g (14oz) can plum tomatoes, chopped
1 tsp basil
60g (2oz) butter or margarine
Salt and pepper

Cook pasta spirals in plenty of boiling salted water for 10 minutes

This page: Pasta Spirals with Peas and Tomatoes.

or until tender. Drain. Meanwhile, cook peas in boiling water with a pinch of salt and a teaspoon of sugar. Melt butter in a pan. Add basil, and cook for 30 seconds.

Add tomatoes and their juice. When hot, add pasta spirals and peas, and salt and pepper to taste. Toss together. Serve immediately.

Tagliatelle with Garlic and Oil

PREPARATION TIME: 5 minutes

COOKING TIME: 10 minutes

300g (10oz) green tagliatelle
150ml (¼ pint) olive oil
3 cloves garlic, crushed
2 tbsps chopped parsley
Salt and pepper

Cook the tagliatelle in lots of boiling salted water for 10 minutes, or until tender but still firm, stirring

This page: Tagliatelle with Garlic and Oil (top) and Spaghetti with Basil Sauce (Pesto) (bottom). Facing page: Noodles with Kidney Beans and Pesto (top) and Cucumber with Yogurt, Dill and Burghul (bottom).

occasionally. Meanwhile, make the sauce. Heat the oil in a pan and,

when warm, add peeled, crushed garlic. Fry gently until golden brown. Add chopped parsley, and salt and pepper to taste. Drain tagliatelle. Add sauce, and toss to coat well. Serve hot.

Black Eye Beans with Curry Dressing

PREPARATION TIME: 10-15 minutes

COOKING TIME: 35-40 minutes

SERVES: 4 people

225g (8oz) black eye beans, soaked overnight
Salt and freshly ground black pepper to taste
1 small onion, thinly sliced
1 green pepper, seeded and finely chopped
Juice of ½ lemon
30ml (2 tblsp) cashew nuts, whole or roughly chopped

Dressing
150ml (¼ pint) natural yogurt
10ml (2 tsp) curry powder
30ml (2 tblsp) fresh pineapple juice
1 clove garlic, crushed

Garnish
Curry powder

Black Eye Beans with Curry Dressing (far left) and Noodles with Fresh Tomato Sauce (above left).

Simmer the beans in salted water until tender. Drain. Mix the black eye beans with the onion and green pepper. Stir in the lemon juice, salt and pepper to taste and the cashew nuts. For the dressing: mix all the ingredients together, adding salt and pepper to taste. Spoon the bean salad into a bowl, and spoon the prepared dressing over the top. Sprinkle with curry powder.

Noodles with Fresh Tomato Sauce

PREPARATION TIME: 10-15 minutes

COOKING TIME: 6-8 minutes

SERVES: 4 people

450g (1lb) tomatoes, skinned and roughly chopped
1 small onion, peeled and chopped
1 clove garlic, peeled and chopped
15ml (1 tblsp) chopped parsley
15ml (1 tblsp) chopped basil
200ml (⅓ pint) olive oil
Salt and freshly ground black pepper to taste
350g (12oz) noodles (green, yellow, or wholemeal)

Garnish
Sprigs fresh basil

Put the tomatoes, onion, garlic, herbs, olive oil, and salt and pepper to taste into the liquidiser and blend until smooth. Cook the noodles in boiling salted water until just tender. Drain thoroughly. Toss the cooked noodles in the prepared tomato sauce. Garnish with sprigs of fresh basil and serve immediately.

Cucumber with Yogurt, Dill and Burghul

PREPARATION TIME: 25 minutes

SERVES: 4 people

90ml (6 tblsp) burghul
1 clove garlic, peeled and crushed
Juice of 1 lemon
60ml (4 tblsp) olive oil
15ml (1 tblsp) fresh dill
Salt and freshly ground black pepper to taste
½ a large cucumber, halved, seeded and chopped
30ml (2 tblsp) natural yogurt

Garnish
Coarsely grated lemon rind
Sprigs of fresh dill

Soak the burghul in sufficient warm water to cover, for 10 minutes. Squeeze the drained burghul in a clean cloth to remove excess moisture. Mix the prepared burghul with the garlic, lemon juice, oil, dill and salt and pepper to taste. Stir in the cucumber and the yogurt. Spoon into a serving dish and garnish with lemon rind and dill.
Note: instead of mixing the yogurt into the burghul, make a well in the centre of the prepared burghul and spoon the yogurt into the centre.

Noodles with Kidney Beans and Pesto

PREPARATION TIME: 5 minutes

COOKING TIME: about 10 minutes

SERVES: 4 people

225g (8oz) wholemeal or plain noodles
Salt and freshly ground black pepper to taste
1 small onion, finely chopped
30ml (2 tblsp) olive oil
1 clove garlic, peeled and crushed
10ml (2 tsp) Pesto sauce (see recipe)
225g (8oz) cooked red kidney beans

Garnish
Sprigs fresh basil

Cook the noodles in a large pan of boiling salted water until just tender. Meanwhile, fry the onion gently in the olive oil for 3 minutes; mix in the garlic and Pesto sauce. Drain the cooked noodles thoroughly; add to the onion and pesto mixture, together with the red kidney beans. Stir over a gentle heat for 1-2 minutes and serve piping hot, garnished with basil.

Spaghetti with Basil Sauce (Pesto)

PREPARATION TIME: 5 minutes

COOKING TIME: 15 minutes

300g (10oz) spaghetti
2 cups fresh basil leaves
2 tbsps pine nuts
75ml (5 tbsps) olive oil
2 cloves garlic, peeled
Salt and pepper
3 tbsps Parmesan or pecorino cheese, grated

Garnish:
Fresh basil

Wash basil and remove leaves, discarding stems. Heat 1 tablespoon of oil over a low temperature. Add garlic and pine nuts, and cook until pine nuts are a light golden brown. Drain. Finely chop basil leaves, pine nuts and garlic in a food processor with a metal blade, or in a blender. When smooth, add remaining oil in a thin stream, blending continuously. Turn mixture into a bowl;

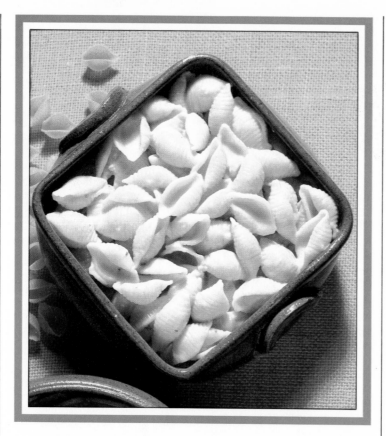

Rinse the mushrooms and chop them roughly. Melt butter in a saucepan and add mushrooms. Fry for 5 minutes, stirring occasionally. Stir in the flour and cook for 1 minute. Draw off the heat, and add milk gradually, stirring continuously. Bring to the boil and cook for 3 minutes. Season with salt and pepper. Meanwhile, cook the pasta shells in lots of boiling salted water for 10 minutes, or until tender but still firm. Rinse in hot water and drain well. Place in a warmed serving dish, and pour over mushroom sauce. Serve immediately.

Farfalle with Tomato Sauce

PREPARATION TIME: 10 minutes
COOKING TIME: 30 minutes

300g (10oz) farfalle
2 400g (14oz) can plum tomatoes, chopped
15ml (1 tbsp) olive oil
1 onion, peeled and sliced
2 cloves garlic, crushed
½ tsp dry basil
Salt and pepper
2 tbsps chopped fresh basil or chopped parsley
Parmesan cheese, grated

Heat oil in a deep pan. Add garlic and onion, and cook until softened. Add dry basil, and cook for 30 seconds. Add undrained tomatoes; season with salt and pepper. Bring to the boil, reduce heat, and simmer, uncovered, for about 20 minutes, or until sauce is reduced by half. Meanwhile, cook the pasta in a large pan of boiling salted water, until tender but still firm – about 10 minutes. Rinse in

mix in grated cheese, and add salt and pepper to taste. Meanwhile, cook spaghetti in a large pan of boiling salted water for 10 minutes, or until just tender. Drain, and serve with basil sauce tossed through. Serve with side dish of grated cheese. Garnish with fresh basil.

Pasta Shells with Gorgonzola Cheese Sauce

PREPARATION TIME: 5 minutes
COOKING TIME: 15 minutes

175g (6oz) gorgonzola cheese
60ml (4 tbsps) milk
30g (1oz) butter or margarine
45ml (3 tbsps) double cream
300g (10oz) shell pasta
Salt
Parmesan cheese, grated

Heat gorgonzola cheese, milk and butter gently in a pan. Stir to a sauce with a wooden spoon. Stir in double cream. Add salt if necessary. Meanwhile, cook shells in plenty of boiling salted water for 10 minutes, or until shells are tender but still firm. Drain, shaking colander to remove excess water. Add shells to hot sauce and toss to coat well. Serve immediately with grated Parmesan cheese on the side.

Pasta Shells with Mushroom Sauce

PREPARATION TIME: 5 minutes
COOKING TIME: 15 minutes

300g (10oz) pasta shells
225g (8oz) button mushrooms
30g (1oz) butter or margarine
15g (½oz) flour
600ml (1 pint) milk
Salt and pepper

This page: Pasta Shells with Gorgonzola Cheese Sauce. Facing page: Pasta Shells with Mushroom Sauce (top) and Farfalle with Tomato Sauce (bottom).

hot water, and drain well. Put sauce through a sieve, and stir in the fresh parsley or basil. Toss sauce through pasta. Serve with grated Parmesan cheese. Serve immediately.

Skillet Rice Cake

| **PREPARATION TIME:** 25 minutes |
| **COOKING TIME:** about 15 minutes |

SERVES: 4 people

1 medium onion, thinly sliced or chopped
1 clove garlic, peeled and chopped
30ml (2 tblsp) olive oil
15ml (1 tblsp) chopped fresh thyme
1 red pepper, seeded and thinly sliced
1 green pepper, seeded and thinly sliced
4 eggs
Salt and freshly ground black pepper to taste

This page: Rice and Vegetable Loaf with Yogurt and Mint Sauce (top) and Skillet Rice Cake (bottom). Facing page: Pasta Shells with Agliata Sauce (top) and Noodle and Ratatouille Bake (bottom).

90ml (6 tblsp) cooked brown or wild rice
45ml (3 tblsp) natural yogurt
75g (3oz) grated cheese

44

Garnish
Chopped fresh thyme

Fry the chopped onion and garlic gently in the olive oil in a frying pan for 3 minutes. Add the thyme and sliced peppers and fry gently for a further 4-5 minutes. Beat the eggs with salt and pepper to taste. Add the cooked rice to the fried vegetables and then add the beaten egg; cook over a moderate heat, stirring from time to time, until the egg starts to set underneath. Spoon the yogurt over the top of the par-set egg and sprinkle with the cheese. Place under a moderately hot grill until puffed and golden. Serve immediately, straight from the pan.

Lobia Curry
(BLACK EYED LOBIA BEAN CURRY)

PREPARATION TIME: soak overnight and 10 minutes

COOKING TIME: 30-40 minutes

225g (8oz) lobia beans, washed and
    soaked overnight in water
600ml (1 pint) water
1 onion, peeled and chopped
50g (2oz) ghee or
45ml (3 tblsp) oil
1 bayleaf
2.5 (1 inch) cinnamon stick
5ml (1 tsp) ginger paste
5ml (1 tsp) garlic paste
1.25ml (¼ tsp) turmeric powder
5ml (1 tsp) ground coriander
5ml (1 tsp) chilli powder
4-5 canned tomatoes, crushed or
4 fresh tomatoes, chopped
Salt to taste
2 green chillis, halved and chopped
2 sprigs fresh coriander leaves,
    chopped

Boil presoaked lobia beans in 600ml (1 pint) water for 20 minutes. Cool. Fry onion in ghee or oil for 3-4 minutes. Add bayleaf, cinnamon, ginger and garlic paste and fry for 2 minutes. Add turmeric, ground coriander, chilli powder and stir the mixture well.

Add boiled lobia and tomatoes. Add salt, chopped chilli and fresh coriander leaves. Cover and cook for 10-15 minutes on gentle heat. The gravy should be of thick consistency. Serve with rice or rotis.

Razma
(RED KIDNEY BEAN CURRY)

PREPARATION TIME: razma to be soaked overnight

COOKING TIME: 40-50 minutes

225g (8oz) red kidney beans, washed
600ml (1 pint) water
5ml (1 tsp) bicarbonate of soda
50g (2oz) ghee or
45ml (3 tblsp) oil
1 onion, peeled and chopped
2.5cm (1 inch) cinnamon stick
1 bayleaf
3 black cardamoms
5ml (1 tsp) ginger paste
5ml (1 tsp) garlic paste
5ml (1 tsp) chilli powder
5ml (1 tsp) ground coriander
5ml (1 tsp) garam masala powder
1.25ml (¼ tsp) turmeric
200g (7-8oz) canned tomatoes,
    crushed
Salt to taste
2 green chillis, halved
2 sprigs fresh coriander leaves,
    chopped

Soak kidney beans in 600ml (1 pint) water with bicarbonate of soda overnight. Next day pressure-cook in 450ml (¾ pint) fresh water (add extra water if some has been absorbed by the beans) for 5-8 minutes. Cool and strain, retaining the liquid. Heat ghee or oil and fry onion for 2-3 minutes. Add cinnamon, bayleaf, cardamoms, ginger and garlic pastes. Cook for 1 minute. Add chilli powder, ground coriander, garam masala and turmeric. Stir the spices well. Add tomatoes and salt. Add kidney beans and fry the mixture for 2-3 minutes. Add 175-250ml (6-8 fl oz) cooking liquid. Sprinkle with green chilli and fresh coriander leaves.

Simmer for 15-20 minutes. Add liquid if gravy is too thick. Remove from heat and serve.

Channa
(CHICKPEA)

PREPARATION TIME: soaking overnight

COOKING TIME: 20-30 minutes

225g (8oz) chickpea
1.3 litres (2¼ pints) water
5ml (1 tsp) bicarbonate of soda
50g (2oz) ghee or
45ml (3 tblsp) oil
1 onion, peeled and chopped
1 bayleaf
2.5cm (1 inch) cinnamon stick
4 black cardamoms
5ml (1 tsp) ginger paste
5ml (1 tsp) garlic paste
5ml (1 tsp) ground coriander
5ml (1 tsp) chilli powder
1.25ml (¼ tsp) turmeric
5 fresh tomatoes, chopped or
5 canned tomatoes, chopped
1-2 green chillis, cut in half
Salt to taste
2 sprigs fresh coriander, chopped

Soak chickpeas overnight in 750ml (1¼ pints) water with the bicarbonate of soda. Drain chickpeas and boil in 600ml (1 pint) of water for 10-12 minutes in a pressure cooker. Strain and save the liquid. Heat ghee or oil and add onion, bayleaf, cinnamon and cardamoms. Fry for 1-2 minutes. Add ginger and garlic pastes. Fry for 1 minute. Sprinkle with coriander, chilli and turmeric powder. Mix well and fry for half a minute. Add tomatoes, green chillis and chickpeas. Mix well and add 175-250ml (6-8 fl oz) cooking liquid. Add extra water if insufficient liquid. Cover and gently simmer for 10-15 minutes.

Facing page: Lobia Curry (top), Razma (centre) and Channa (bottom).

Add salt and green coriander. The chickpeas should disintegrate when pressed between thumb and index finger. If not fully tender add extra water and cook further. Channa is a thick, moist dish. Serve with kulcha or nan.

Pasta Shells with Agliata Sauce

PREPARATION TIME: 10 minutes

COOKING TIME: about 8 minutes

SERVES: 4 people

275g (10oz) wholemeal or plain pasta shells
Salt and freshly ground black pepper to taste

Sauce
90ml (6 tblsp) olive oil
45ml (3 tblsp) coarsely chopped parsley
2 cloves garlic, peeled
15ml (1 tblsp) pine kernels
15ml (1 tblsp) blanched almonds

Cook the pasta shells in a large pan of boiling salted water until just tender. Meanwhile, make the sauce. Put all the ingredients into a liquidiser and blend until smooth; add salt and pepper to taste. Drain the hot, cooked pasta shells and toss together with the prepared sauce. Serve immediately.

Chick Pea, Mint and Orange Salad

PREPARATION TIME: 15-25 minutes

SERVES: 4 people

175g (6oz) dried chick peas, soaked overnight and cooked
30ml (2 tblsp) chopped fresh mint
1 clove garlic, peeled and crushed
Salt and freshly ground black pepper to taste
Juice of 1 orange

Rind of 1 orange, cut into matchstick strips
45ml (3 tblsp) olive oil
Segments from 2 large oranges

Garnish
Fresh mint leaves

Mix the chick peas with half the chopped mint, garlic, and salt and pepper to taste. Mix the orange juice, strips of orange rind and olive oil together; stir into the chick peas. Lightly mix in the orange segments and garnish with the remaining chopped mint.

Spinach and Feta Cheese Lasagne

PREPARATION TIME: 20-25 minutes

COOKING TIME: about 35 minutes

OVEN: 190°, 375°F, Gas Mark 5

SERVES: 6 people

450g (1lb) cooked and drained spinach (or thawed frozen spinach)
Generous pinch grated nutmeg
Salt and freshly ground black pepper to taste
30ml (2 tblsp) natural yogurt
1 clove garlic, peeled and crushed
1 egg yolk
175g (6oz) Feta cheese, crumbled
225g (8oz) green or wholewheat lasagne (the non pre-cook variety)

Sauce
150ml (¼ pint) natural yogurt
1 egg, beaten
30ml (2 tblsp) grated Parmesan cheese
3 firm tomatoes, sliced

Mix the cooked spinach with nutmeg and salt and pepper to taste; stir in the yogurt, garlic, egg yolk and crumbled Feta cheese. Layer the lasagne and spinach mixture in a lightly greased ovenproof dish, starting with spinach and finishing with lasagne. For the sauce: mix the yogurt with

the beaten egg and half the grated Parmesan cheese; spoon over the lasagne. Top with the sliced tomato and the remaining Parmesan cheese. Bake in the oven for about 35 minutes, until golden. Serve piping hot.

Rice and Vegetable Loaf with Yogurt and Mint Sauce

PREPARATION TIME: 25-30 minutes

COOKING TIME: 53 minutes

OVEN: 190°C, 375°F, Gas Mark 5

SERVES: 6-8

1 small onion, finely chopped
30ml (2 tblsp) olive oil
1 clove garlic, peeled and crushed
225g (8oz) wild rice, cooked and drained (not rinsed)
3 courgettes, finely shredded
2 medium size carrots, finely shredded
30ml (2 tblsp) chopped parsley
Salt and freshly ground black pepper to taste
5ml (1 tsp) chopped fresh thyme
2-3 eggs, beaten
75g (3oz) grated cheese

Garnish
Fresh mint

Fry the onion gently in the olive oil for 3 minutes. Mix together with all the remaining ingredients, adding sufficient beaten egg to give a stiff yet moist consistency. Spoon the mixture into a deep, greased and lined loaf tin, smoothing the surface level. Cover with a piece of lightly greased foil. Bake in the oven for 50 minutes. Allow to cool slightly in the tin before turning out. Serve the rice and vegetable loaf cut into slices, and accompanied by the yogurt and mint sauce. Garnish with mint. For the sauce: mix 150ml (¼ pint) natural yogurt with salt and freshly ground black pepper to taste and 15ml (1 tblsp) chopped mint.

Noodle and Ratatouille Bake

PREPARATION TIME: 25-30 minutes

COOKING TIME: 35-40 minutes

OVEN: 190°C, 375°F, Gas Mark 5

SERVES: 4 people

1 medium onion, thinly sliced
30ml (2 tblsp) olive oil
2 cloves garlic, peeled and finely chopped
1 large green pepper, seeded and cut into cubes
1 large red pepper, seeded and cut into cubes
1 medium aubergine, cubed
6 tomatoes, skinned, seeded and

This page: Chick Pea, Mint and Orange Salad (top) and Spinach and Feta Cheese Lasagne (bottom).

chopped
15ml (1 tblsp) tomato puree
45ml (3 tblsp) red wine
Salt and freshly ground black pepper

to taste
100g (4oz) green noodles, cooked
75g (3oz) grated cheese

Fry the onion gently in the olive oil for 4 minutes; add the garlic, red and green peppers, aubergine and chopped tomatoes and cook covered for 5 minutes. Add the tomato puree, wine and salt and pepper to taste; simmer gently for 10-15 minutes, until the vegetables are almost soft. Remove from the heat and stir in the cooked noodles. Spoon into a shallow flameproof dish and sprinkle with the grated cheese. Bake in the oven for 15 minutes (alternatively, the dish can be flashed under a preheated grill).

Spaghetti Neapolitana

PREPARATION TIME: 5 minutes	
COOKING TIME: 30 minutes	
SERVES: 4 people	

300g (10oz) spaghetti
2 400g (14oz) cans plum tomatoes
30ml (2 tbsps) olive oil
½ tsp oregano or marjoram
Salt
Pepper
2 tbsps chopped parsley
Parmesan cheese, grated

Push undrained tomatoes through a sieve. Heat oil in pan. Add oregano or marjoram, and cook for 30 seconds. Add puréed tomatoes, and salt and pepper. Bring to boil;

This page: Gianfottere Salad. Facing page: Spaghetti Neapolitana (top) and Farfalle with Creamy Cheese Sauce (bottom).

reduce heat; simmer uncovered for 20-30 minutes. Meanwhile, cook spaghetti in lots of boiling salted water for about 10 minutes, or until tender but still firm. Rinse under hot water, and drain well. Pour tomato sauce over spaghetti, and toss gently. Sprinkle parsley over the top. Serve with Parmesan cheese. Serve immediately.

Gianfottere Salad

PREPARATION TIME: 40 minutes

COOKING TIME: 30 minutes

SERVES: 4 people

225g (8oz) pasta spirals
1 aubergine (egg plant)
1 courgette (zucchini)
1 red pepper
1 green pepper
2 tomatoes
1 onion
60ml (4 tbsps) olive oil
1 clove garlic
Salt
Pepper

Cut aubergine into 1cm (½") slices. Sprinkle with salt and leave for 30 minutes. Skin the tomatoes by putting them into boiling water for 20 seconds, and then rinsing in cold water, and peeling skins off. Chop roughly. Cut courgette into 1cm (½") slices. Remove cores and seeds from peppers, and chop roughly. Peel and chop onion. Heat 45ml (3 tbsps) olive oil in pan, and fry onion gently until transparent, but not coloured. Meanwhile, rinse salt from aubergine, and pat dry with absorbent paper. Chop roughly. Add aubergine, courgette, peppers, tomatoes and garlic to onion, and fry gently for 20 minutes. Season with salt and pepper. Allow to cool. Meanwhile, cook pasta spirals in a lot of boiling salted water for 10 minutes, or until tender but still firm. Rinse in cold water and drain well, and toss in remaining 15ml (1 tbsp) olive oil. Toss vegetables together with pasta spirals.

Farfalle with Creamy Cheese Sauce

PREPARATION TIME: 5 minutes

COOKING TIME: 15 minutes

SERVES: 4 people

300g (10oz) farfalle (pasta butterflies /bows)
15g (½ oz) butter or margarine
15g (½ oz) flour
300ml (½ pint) milk
60g (2oz) Gruyère or Cheddar cheese, grated
½ tsp French mustard
1 tbsp grated Parmesan cheese

Heat butter in pan. Stir in flour and cook for 1 minute. Remove from heat and gradually stir in milk. Return to heat and stir continuously. Boil for 3 minutes. Stir in Gruyère or Cheddar cheese, and mustard; do not reboil. Meanwhile, cook the pasta in lots of boiling salted water for 10 minutes, or until tender but still firm. Rinse in hot water and drain well. Pour over cheese sauce, and toss. Top with a sprinkling of Parmesan cheese. Serve immediately.

Chapter Four

MAIN COURSES

Ginger Cauliflower

This is a very simple and extremely subtle vegetable dish spiced with ginger.

PREPARATION TIME: 15 minutes

COOKING TIME: 15 minutes

SERVES: 4 people

45ml (3 tblsp) oil
1 medium onion, peeled and chopped
2.5cm (1 inch) fresh root ginger, peeled and sliced
1-2 green chillies, cut in half lengthways
1 medium cauliflower, cut into 2.5cm (1 inch) florets, along with tender leaves and stalk
Salt to taste
2-3 sprigs fresh green coriander leaves, chopped
Juice of 1 lemon

Heat the oil in a wok or solid based saucepan; fry the onion, ginger and chillies for 2-3 minutes. Add the cauliflower and salt to taste. Stir to mix well. Cover and cook over a low heat for 5-6 minutes. Add the coriander leaves and cook for a further 2-3 minutes, or until the florets of cauliflower are tender. Sprinkle with lemon juice, mix well and serve immediately. Serve with pitta bread.

Facing page: Ginger Cauliflower (top left), Mixed Vegetable Raita (top right) and Cannelloni with Spinach and Ricotta (bottom).

Spiced Chick Peas

This dryish curry is a "must" on any Punjabi menu. It is usually served with milk bread or pitta bread and an onion salad.

PREPARATION TIME: overnight	overnight for soaking, plus 15 minutes
COOKING TIME:	40-50 minutes
SERVES:	4-6 people

450g (1lb) chick peas
5ml (1 tsp) baking powder
4 cloves
5ml (1 tsp) cumin seed
4 large black cardamoms, ground
4 small cardamoms, ground
1 large onion, peeled and chopped
45ml (3 tblsp) oil
2 bayleaves
2.5cm (1 inch) piece cinnamon stick
2 green chillies, sliced in half lengthways
2.5cm (1 inch) fresh root ginger, peeled and finely chopped
4 cloves garlic, peeled and crushed
7.5ml (1½ tsp) ground coriander
250-300ml (8-10 fl oz) canned tomatoes, chopped
2.5ml (½ tp) freshly ground black pepper
2.5ml (½ tsp) salt
5-6 sprigs fresh green coriander leaves, chopped

Wash the chick peas and soak them overnight in 1.2 litres (2 pints) water and the baking powder. The following day, cook the chick peas in their soaking liquid in a pressure cooker for 10-15 minutes. If a lot of liquid has been absorbed during soaking, add a little more. Dry roast the cloves and cumin seed in a frying pan. Grind the cloves, cumin, large and small cardamons into a fine powder. Fry the onion in the oil for 2-3 minutes. Add the bayleaves, cinnamon, chillies, ginger and garlic. Fry for 1 minute, add the ground coriander and tomatoes. Fry for 2-3 minutes. Strain the chick peas, retaining any liquid. Add the chick peas to the tomato mixture and add black pepper, salt and the dry roasted spices. Mix well and add 250ml (8 fl oz) of the strained chick pea liquid. Sprinkle with chopped coriander; cover and cook for 8-10 minutes. Add a little extra liquid if necessary. Serve with bread or rice.

Vegetable Pancakes

A combination of shredded vegetables makes a delicious pancake, when added to the batter before cooking.

Vegetable Pancakes (far left) and Spiced Chick Peas (left).

PREPARATION TIME: 15 minutes

COOKING TIME: 15 minutes

SERVES: 4-6 people

100g (4oz) butter
225g (8oz) shredded or coarsely grated carrots
225g (8oz) shredded or coarsely grated courgettes
450g (1lb) shredded or coarsely grated potatoes
1 medium onion, thinly sliced
3 eggs, well beaten
200ml (⅓ pint) soured cream
60ml (4 tblsp) cornflour
2.5ml (½ tsp) salt
2.5ml (½ tsp) freshly ground black pepper
Oil for frying
Wedges of lemon

Melt the butter in a frying pan; add the carrots, courgettes, potatoes and onion. Sauté for 3-4 minutes, stirring continuously. Beat the eggs together with the soured cream, cornflour and salt and pepper. Mix well. Stir in the semi-cooked vegetables. Mix together gently. Heat a large non-stick frying pan and brush with 10ml (2 tsp) oil; add 15ml (1 tblsp) batter. Cook until light brown; turn the small pancake over and cook until the other side is also brown. Make 3 or 4 at a time. The size of the pancakes can be increased by using more batter for each pancake. Serve with salads or with tomato sauce as a light meal or snack.

New Potato Fry

This Oriental dish is very versatile; it can be served as a side dish, as a snack, or as a main curry.

PREPARATION TIME: 20 minutes

COOKING TIME: 10-12 minutes

SERVES: 3-4 people

45ml (3 tblsp) oil
5ml (1 tsp) mustard seed
450g (1lb) small, even sized new potatoes, boiled in their skins and peeled

5ml (1 tsp) red chilli powder
7.5ml (1½ tsp) ground coriander
1.25ml (¼ tsp) ground turmeric
2.5ml (½ tsp) salt
3 sprigs fresh green coriander leaves, chopped (optional)
Lemon juice to taste

Heat the oil in a wok or solid based frying pan and add the mustard seed and the whole, peeled potatoes. Stir fry over a low heat until they are lightly browned. Sprinkle with the spices, salt and chopped coriander leaves. Stir fry over a low heat for 5-6 minutes until golden brown. Remove from heat. Put into a dish and sprinkle with the lemon juice. Serve hot or cold.

Spinach with Paneer

Paneer is a home-made cheese; it is made by separating milk into curds and whey by means of a souring agent such as lemon juice. It is eaten extensively in northern parts of India and is a good source of protein.

PREPARATION TIME: 15 minutes, plus time for making paneer

COOKING TIME: 20-30 minutes

SERVES: 4 people

To make paneer: (This is an overnight process)
1.2 litres (2 pints) milk
30ml (2 tblsp) lemon juice

Bring the milk to the boil. Reduce the heat and sprinkle with the lemon juice. The milk will separate into pale watery whey and thick white paneer (or curds). Remove from the heat and allow the paneer to coagulate (if the milk has not separated properly, add a few more drops of lemon juice. The whey should be a clear, pale, yellow liquid. Pour the paneer and liquid through a muslin-lined sieve. Discard the liquid whey and tie the muslin over the paneer. Flatten the paneer to 1cm (½ inch) thick; place it on a tray and rest it in a

tilted position. Place more muslin over the top and weight it down. The pressure will drag out the remaining moisture and the tilted position will channel the liquid away from the paneer. Leave to drain overnight. Next day, cut the firm paneer into 2.5cm (1 inch) cubes.

75g (3oz) butter
1 medium onion, peeled and finely chopped
2.5cm (1 inch) piece cinnamon stick
1 bayleaf
450g (1lb) frozen spinach puree, or fresh leaf spinach, cooked and pureed
5ml (1 tsp) chilli powder
2.5ml (½ tsp) salt
120g (4½oz) natural yogurt
3 sprigs fresh green coriander leaves, chopped
5ml (1 tsp) garam masala powder
Oil for deep frying

Heat the butter in a pan and fry the onion until golden brown. Add the cinnamon and bayleaf and fry for 1 minute. Add the spinach and stir to mix. Sprinkle with the chilli powder and salt and stir in the yogurt, coriander leaves and garam masala. Cover and cook for 2-3 minutes. Simmer gently. Meanwhile, deep-fry the drained paneer cubes until golden. Add the paneer cubes to the spinach and simmer together for 4-5 minutes. Serve hot with chapati or pulao rice.

Spiced Peas

PREPARATION TIME: 10 minutes

COOKING TIME: 15 minutes

SERVES: 6 people

30ml (2 tblsp) oil
1 large onion, peeled and chopped

Facing page: Spiced Peas (top), Spinach with Paneer (centre) and New Potato Fry (bottom).

2 green chillies, sliced in half
    lengthways
1kg (2lb) shelled peas (fresh or
    frozen)
Salt and freshly ground black pepper
    to taste
15ml (1 tblsp) lemon juice
Lemon wedges

Heat the oil in a wok or solid based
frying pan and fry the onion until
tender. Add the chillies and fry for
1 minute. Add the peas and salt
and pepper to taste; stir fry for 5-
10 minutes, or until well coloured
and "dry". Put into a serving dish

and sprinkle with lemon juice.
Garnish with lemon wedges. Serve
as a side dish, or as a snack.

Egg and Potato Omelette

50g (2oz) butter
2 small cooked potatoes, diced
4 eggs
2.5ml (½ tsp) salt
Pinch of pepper

Heat the butter in a frying or
omelette pan. Add the potatoes
and cook until golden. Beat the

**This page: Mung Fritters.
Facing page: Cheese Bread
Pudding (centre left) and
Egg and Potato Omelette
(bottom).**

eggs and season. Add the eggs to
the potato and cook quickly until
the mixture is set. Fold over and
serve at once. Serve with a green
vegetable.

Mung Fritters

These tiny marble-sized fritters are made with mung pulse. They can be eaten as a cocktail snack or made into a curry with a well-flavoured sauce.

PREPARATION TIME: 1 hour 30 minutes

COOKING TIME: 30 minutes

SERVES: 4 people

225g (8oz) split mung pulse
1 small onion, peeled and chopped
5ml (1 tsp) chilli powder
7.5ml (1½ tsp) garam masala powder
2.5ml (½ tsp) cumin seed
4-5 sprigs fresh green coriander leaves, chopped
2.5ml (½ tsp) salt
Oil for deep frying

Wash and soak the mung pulse for 1 hour in sufficient cold water to cover. Drain and then grind into a thick coarse paste, adding 120-250ml (4-8 fl oz) water as you go. It should be the consistency of peanut butter. Mix the mung paste with the onion, chilli powder, garam masala, cumin seed, coriander leaves and salt. Mix well and adjust seasoning if necessary. Heat the oil for deep frying. Using a teaspoon, shape the paste into small "marbles" and fry in the hot oil until golden brown. Drain on kitchen paper and serve piping hot with chutney, a chilli sauce or a dip. To turn into a curry, add the Mung Fritters to the following curry sauce.

Sauce
10ml (2 tsp) oil
1 small onion, finely chopped

2.5ml (½ tsp) chilli powder
5ml (1 tsp) ground coriander
5ml (1 tsp) ground cumin
4-6 canned tomatoes, chopped
Salt to taste
3-4 sprigs fresh green coriander
    leaves, chopped

Heat the oil in a saucepan and fry
the onion for 3 minutes. Stir in all
the above ingredients; cover and
simmer for 5-8 minutes. Add a
little water to make a thickish
sauce. Add ready-fried Mung
Fritters and simmer for 3-5
minutes.

Garlic Hash Brown

| **PREPARATION TIME:** 20 minutes |
| **COOKING TIME:** 30 minutes |
| **SERVES:** 4 people |

60ml (4 tblsp) oil
4 cloves of garlic, peeled and
    quartered lengthways
3 whole red chillies
Salt
450-750g (1-1½lb) potatoes, peeled
    and coarsely grated

Heat the oil in a wok or a large
non-stick frying pan. Fry the garlic
until lightly browned. Add the red
chillies and fry for 30 seconds.
Sprinkle with salt to taste and add
the grated potato. Stir fry for 5
minutes. Cover and cook for a
further 8-10 minutes. The potatoes
should be crisp and golden brown.
Cook until the potatoes are tender.
Serve as a side dish or for breakfast.

Green Beans with Coconut

| **PREPARATION TIME:** 10 minutes |
| **COOKING TIME:** 20 minutes |
| **SERVES:** 3-4 people |

30ml (2 tblsp) oil
2 cloves garlic, peeled and crushed
2 green or red dried chillies
450g (1lb) green beans, sliced

1.25ml (¼ tsp) salt
30ml (2 tblsp) desiccated coconut, or
    grated fresh coconut

Heat the oil in a wok or frying pan.
Add the garlic and fry until golden
brown. Add the chillies and stir fry
for 30 seconds. Add the green
beans and sprinkle with salt. Stir
fry for 8-10 minutes until the beans
are tender but still crisp. Sprinkle
with the coconut and stir fry for a
further 2-3 minutes. Serve as a side
dish.

Noodles with Vegetables

This exotic noodle dish can be
served hot or cold, as a main
course, as a side dish or as a snack.

| **PREPARATION TIME:** 20 minutes |
| **COOKING TIME:** 30 minutes |
| **SERVES:** 4 people |

Salt to taste
450g (1lb) egg noodles, or broken
    spaghetti
45ml (3 tblsp) oil
2.5cm (1 inch) fresh root ginger,
    peeled and thinly sliced
1 large or 2 medium onions, peeled
    and sliced
75g (3oz) green beans, sliced

75g (3oz) carrots, peeled and cut into
    matchstick strips
100g (4oz) white cabbage, or
    Chinese leaves, shredded
50g (2oz) shelled peas
75g (3oz) sprouting mung beans
1 green pepper, seeded and cut into
    2.5cm (1 inch) pieces
1-2 stems celery, chopped
1-2 green chillies, split lengthways
2.5ml (½ tsp) monosodium
    glutamate (optional)
30ml (2 tblsp) soya sauce
15ml (1 tblsp) lemon juice

**Facing page: Noodles with
Vegetables (top left), Green
Beans with Coconut (top
right) and Garlic Hash
Brown (bottom).**

5-10ml (1-2 tsp) Chinese red pepper
  sauce
60ml (4 tblsp) vegetable stock

Bring a large pan of water to the
boil and add 5ml (1 tsp) salt. Add
the noodles or spaghetti and boil
gently for 5-6 minutes. Drain the
noodles. Rinse the noodles in cold
water and drain once again. Heat
the oil in a wok or large frying pan.
Fry the ginger for 1-2 minutes. Add
the onions and fry for 2-3 minutes.
Add the beans and carrots and fry
for 2 minutes. Add the remaining
vegetables and the chillies and stir
fry for 3-4 minutes. Add salt to
taste and the noodles. Stir lightly
with two forks. Dissolve the
monosodium glutamate in the soya
sauce and sprinkle over the noodle
mixture; stir in the lemon juice,
Chinese sauce and stock. Heat
through for 2-3 minutes. Serve hot.

Macaroni Cheese

175g (6oz) quick cooking macaroni
1.75 litre (3 pints) water

Cheese Sauce
40g (1½oz) butter
40g (1½oz) flour
450ml (¾ pint) milk
Salt and pepper
100g (4oz) Cheddar cheese, grated

Topping
25-50g (1-2oz) Cheddar cheese,
  grated
25g (1oz) dried breadcrumbs

Garnish
1 tomato
Parsley

Boil the macaroni in salted water
for about 7 minutes. Add a little
pepper if desired. Melt the butter
in a saucepan, stir in the flour and
cook for 2 minutes. Cool.
Gradually blend in the milk, bring
to the boil and cook until
thickened and smooth. Add
seasoning, and the cheese. Strain
the macaroni and blend with the
sauce. Put into a 1.2 litre (2-pint)
dish, top with the cheese and
breadcrumbs and brown under a
hot grill. Garnish with tomato and
parsley.

Cheese Crust Vegetable Pie

Cheese Pastry
175g (6oz) flour
Pinch of salt
100g (4oz) butter or margarine
75g (3oz) Cheddar cheese, grated
30-45ml (2-3 tblsp) cold water to
  mix

Filling

50g (2oz) butter
1 onion, peeled and sliced
200g (7oz) can sweet corn
3 carrots, peeled and sliced
50g (2oz) mushrooms, sliced
50g (2oz) packet of leek soup
2 sticks celery, scrubbed and sliced
Pepper
1 egg, beaten to glaze

Sift the flour and salt into a mixing bowl. Rub the butter or margarine into the flour and stir in the cheese. Bind together with the water. Melt the butter in a pan and fry the vegetables for a few minutes. Drain on paper towels. Make up the packet of leek soup as directed, but using only 600ml (1 pint) of water. Stir the vegetables into the leek soup, season with pepper and pour into a 900ml (1½ pint) pie dish. Roll out the pastry to top the pie. Trim and flute the edges. Use any leftover pastry to decorate the pie top. Brush with beaten egg. Cook in the oven for 15 minutes at 200°C, 400°F, Gas Mark 6. Reduce the heat to 180°C, 350°F, Gas Mark 4, and cook for a further 20 minutes. Serve with new potatoes.

Cheese Crust Vegetable Pie (top), Cheese and Potato Whirls (far left) and Macaroni Cheese (above left).

Cheese Hot Pot

500g (1¼lb) potatoes
175g (6oz) onions
175g (6oz) carrots
250g (9oz) grated cheese
Salt and pepper
150ml (5 fl oz) water
Chopped parsley to garnish

Peel the potatoes, onions and carrots, and cut into thin slices. Put in layers into a deep dish, with the cheese and a little seasoning between layers. Continue until all the vegetables are used, finishing with a layer of cheese. Pour the water into the dish to moisten. Cover with a greased lid and cook in the oven for 30 minutes at 230°C, 450°F, Gas Mark 8. Reduce to 190°C, 375°F, Gas Mark 5, and cook for a further 1½ hours. Remove the lid and allow to brown for about 5 minutes. Garnish with chopped parsley.

Mixed Vegetable Raita

Raitas are yogurt-based Indian dishes served as accompaniments to curries etc. Natural yogurt is usually mixed with fruits, vegetables, and herbs such as coriander or mint.

PREPARATION TIME: 10 minutes
SERVES: 4-6 people

300ml (½ pint) natural yogurt
½ cucumber, chopped
1 small onion, peeled and chopped
2 tomatoes, chopped
2 stems celery, chopped
1 small apple, cored and chopped
2 boiled potatoes, peeled and chopped
1.25ml (¼ tsp) salt
1.25ml (¼ tsp) freshly ground black pepper
1 sprig fresh green coriander, chopped

Beat the yogurt in a bowl. Add all the remaining ingredients, seasoning well with salt and pepper. Chill before serving.

Cheese Bread Pudding

4 large slices of buttered bread
100-175g (4-6oz) Cheddar cheese, grated
Salt and pepper
5ml (1 tsp) soy sauce
Pinch of dry mustard
2 eggs
450ml (¾ pint) milk

Cut the crusts off the bread and cut each slice into 6 squares. Fill a greased, 900ml (1½ pint) pie dish with layers of bread, cheese, seasoning, soy sauce and mustard. Reserve a little cheese. Beat together the eggs and milk and pour over the layers. Sprinkle the top with the reserved cheese and cook in the oven for 40-45 minutes at 160°C, 325°F, Gas Mark 3. Serve with potato croquettes.

Cannelloni with Spinach and Ricotta

PREPARATION TIME: 20 minutes
COOKING TIME: 1 hour 20 minutes
SERVES: 4 people

30ml (2 tblsp) olive oil or melted butter
1 large onion, peeled and finely chopped
2 large cloves garlic, peeled and crushed
425g (15oz) can peeled tomatoes, chopped
15ml (1 tblsp) tomato puree
Salt and freshly ground black pepper to taste
7.5ml (1½ tsp) dried basil
2.5ml (½ tsp) dried oregano
350g (12oz) cannelloni tubes
60ml (4 tblsp) thick spinach puree
225g (8oz) Ricotta cheese
30ml (2 tblsp) grated Parmesan cheese

To make the sauce: heat the oil or butter and fry the onion and garlic for 2-3 minutes. Add the tomatoes

and tomato puree and mix well. Simmer for 2 minutes. Add the salt and pepper, basil and oregano. Cover and simmer for 10-15 minutes until thick.

Bring a large pan of salted water to the boil; cook the cannelloni tubes for 10 minutes until just tender. Do not overboil. Lift out the cannelloni tubes and put them into a bowl of cold water to cool quickly. Drain well. Mix together the spinach, ricotta and salt and pepper to taste. Fill the cannelloni tubes with the spinach mixture and arrange them in a greased shallow ovenproof dish. Pour the tomato sauce over the cannelloni; sprinkle with the Parmesan cheese. Bake for 20-30 minutes at 180°C, 350°F, Gas Mark 4 or until the top is browned and bubbling. Serve at once.

Cheese and Potato Whirls

100g (¼lb) instant potato powder or 1lb of potatoes, cooked
25g (1oz) butter and a little milk, if using cooked potatoes
450g (1lb) grated cheese
1 egg
Salt and pepper
Mixed mustard
Egg, beaten to glaze

Rough Puff Pastry
225g (½lb) plain flour
2.5ml (½ tsp) salt
175g (6oz) margarine
10ml (2 tsp) wine vinegar or lemon juice
150ml (¼ pint) ice-cold water

First make the pastry. Sieve the flour and salt into a bowl. Cut margarine into 1cm (½") dice. Toss through the flour. Add vinegar or lemon juice to the water. Add to the flour and mix to a soft dough. Turn on to a floured board. Roll into a square. Fold the side edges to the middle, top and bottom to middle, then fold in half. Press gently together. Leave to rest in refrigerator for 15 minutes. Remove and roll the pastry once again into a square, fold the side edges to the middle, top and bottom to middle, then fold in half. Make the instant potato as directed on the tin or packet or mash the cooked potato with the butter and milk. Add the cheese, egg, seasoning and mustard. Roll the pastry into a square, spread with the cheese and potato mixture. Roll up as for a Swiss roll and brush with egg to glaze. Cut into the required number of slices and cook on a baking tray in the oven for 20-25 minutes at 230°C, 440°F, Gas Mark 8.

Chapter Five
DRINKS AND DESSERTS

Golden Pistachio Meringues

PREPARATION TIME: 15-20 minutes

COOKING TIME: 1 hour

OVEN: 110°C, 225°F, Gas Mark ¼

MAKES: about 6

2 egg whites
100g (4oz) golden granulated sugar

Filling
100g (4oz) curd cheese
15ml (1 tblsp) clear honey
30ml (2 tblsp) chopped shelled
*   pistachios*

To Decorate
Chopped shelled pistachios

Whisk the egg whites until stiff but not dry and then gradually whisk in the golden granulated sugar. Pipe into 6 nest shapes on lightly greased and floured baking sheets. Bake in the oven for 1 hour. The meringues should be fairly crisp

This page: Cinnamon and Peanut Cookies (top) and Golden Pistachio Meringues (bottom).

but they should not 'colour'. Allow to cool. For the filling: cream the cheese until soft; beat in the honey and chopped pistachios. Fill the meringue nests with the cheese filling. Sprinkle each one with extra pistachios.

Cinnamon and Peanut Cookies

PREPARATION TIME: 15-20 minutes

COOKING TIME: 20 minutes

OVEN: 180°C, 350°F, Gas Mark 4

MAKES: about 20

100g (4oz) softened butter
100g (4oz) soft brown sugar
1 egg, beaten
60ml (4 tblsp) clear honey
250g (9oz) wholemeal flour
2.5ml (½ tsp) ground cinnamon
5ml (1 tsp) baking powder
Pinch salt
75g (3oz) shelled peanuts

Cream the butter and sugar until well mixed (do not over-beat). Mix in the beaten egg and honey and then mix in the flour, cinnamon, baking powder and salt. Put heaped teaspoons of the mixture onto greased baking sheets, allowing room for spreading; flatten each one slightly with the rounded side of a dampened spoon. Stud the tops with peanuts. Bake in the oven for 20 minutes.
Note: for really golden topped biscuits bake them as above for just 15 minutes; brush each one with beaten egg and return to the oven for a further 5 minutes.

Carrotella

PREPARATION TIME: 15 minutes

COOKING TIME: 35-40 minutes

SERVES: 4-6 people

1.2 litre (2 pints) milk
450g (1lb) carrots, peeled and shredded

200ml (⅓ pint) canned evaporated milk
100g (4oz) granulated sugar
50g (2oz) raisins
Seeds of 8 small cardamoms, crushed
2 drops rose-water or vanilla essence
50g (2oz) chopped blanched almonds
50g (2oz) pistachio nuts, chopped

Put the milk into a pan and simmer over a low heat until reduced to 900ml (1½ pints). Add the carrots; cover and cook over a medium heat for 15 minutes. Add the evaporated milk, sugar and raisins. Cover and simmer gently for another 5 minutes. Remove from the heat. Stir in the crushed cardamom seeds and essence and pour into a serving dish. Allow to cool slightly. Sprinkle nuts on the top and serve. On hot summer days, the Carrotella is best chilled.

Carrot Cake

PREPARATION TIME: 30 minutes

COOKING TIME: 45-50 minutes

MAKES: 25cm (10 inch) loaf

175g (6oz) butter or margarine
175g (6oz) brown sugar
100g (4oz) granulated sugar
2 eggs, well beaten
225g (8oz) plain flour
7.5ml (1½ tsp) bicarbonate of soda
2.5ml (½ tsp) baking powder
1.25ml (¼ tsp) ground cinnamon
2.5ml (½ tsp) salt
225g (8oz) peeled carrots, shredded
75g (3oz) raisins
50g (2oz) chopped walnuts
1.25ml (¼ tsp) small cardamom seeds, crushed
Icing sugar for dredging

Cream the butter and sugars together. Add the eggs, a little at a time, beating well after each addition. Sieve the flour, bicarbonate of soda, baking powder, cinnamon and salt together. Fold the dry ingredients into the egg mixture. Add the carrots, raisins, nuts and crushed cardamom. Mix well and pour the

mixture into a well buttered 25cm (10 inch) loaf tin. Bake at 180°C, 350°F, Gas Mark 4, for 45-50 minutes, or until a fine metal skewer comes out clean when inserted into the centre of the cake. Cool in the tin for 10-15 minutes, before turning out. Dredge with icing sugar before serving.

Carrot Halva

A delightful sweet from the mysterious East. Serve it hot or cold, with or without cream.

PREPARATION TIME: 20 minutes

COOKING TIME: 50 minutes

SERVES: 8-10 people

2kg (4lb) large sweet carrots, peeled and shredded
900ml (1½ pints) canned evaporated milk
750g (1½lbs) granulated sugar
175g (6oz) unsalted butter
75g (3oz) raisins
Seeds of 10 small cardamoms, crushed
100g (4oz) chopped mixed nuts (blanched and chopped almonds, cashews, pistachios etc.)
Single cream

Put the carrots, evaporated milk and sugar into a large solid based pan and bring to the boil. Reduce the heat and cook the carrots gently for 30-40 minutes, or until the milk has evaporated. Add the butter and raisins and stir over a gentle heat for 8-10 minutes, until the Halva is dark and leaves the sides of the pan clean. Add the cardamom seeds and mix well. Pour into a flat shallow dish about 2.5cm (1 inch) deep. Flatten the Halva evenly with a spatula. Sprinkle with the chopped nuts. Serve hot or cold, cut into squares, with single cream.

Facing page: Carrot Cake (top), Carrot Halva (centre) and Carrotella (bottom).

Tropical Fruit Dessert

An exotic sweet dish to finish any special meal. A delightful dessert from nature's fruit garden.

PREPARATION TIME: 30 minutes

SERVES: 8-10 people

4 bananas, cut into 5mm (¼ inch) thick slices
5 rings pineapple, cut into chunks (fresh or canned)
2 semi-ripe pears, peeled, cored and cut into chunks
2 medium red-skinned apples, cored and cut into chunks
8 peach slices, chopped
225g (8oz) red cherries, pitted
45ml (3 tblsp) grated fresh coconut
1 honeydew melon, peeled and cut into chunks
6-8 slices mango, cut into chunks (fresh or canned)
2 kiwi fruit, peeled and cut into chunks
20-25 strawberries, halved
Few seedless white and black grapes, halved
15ml (1 tblsp) icing sugar
100g (4oz) cottage cheese
Few drops vanilla essence

Mix all the ingredients together in a large bowl. Cover and chill for 1 hour.

Frozen Lemon Yogurt Souffle

PREPARATION TIME: 20 minutes

SERVES: 4-6 people

900ml (1½ pints) natural yogurt
225g (8oz) caster sugar
Juice and finely grated rind of 2 lemons
5ml (1 tsp) vanilla essence
2 egg whites
1.25ml (¼ tsp) salt
1.25ml (¼ tsp) cream of tartar
120ml (4 fl oz) double cream, whipped
Few thin lemon slices for decoration

Mix the yogurt, sugar, lemon juice, lemon rind and vanilla essence together. Whisk the egg whites, salt and cream of tartar until stiff but not dry. Fold the egg whites gently into the yogurt mixture, and then fold in the whipped cream. Pour the mixture into a souffle dish and freeze overnight. Garnish with lemon slices before serving. Serve either frozen or partially thawed.

Tropical Fruit Salad

This medley of fruits is very colourful and it offers a variety of tastes and textures.

PREPARATION TIME: 40 minutes

2 bananas, sliced
4 kiwi fruit, peeled and sliced
10 dates, stoned and sliced in half
2 guavas, halved and then sliced into wedges
1 pawpaw, cut into thin crescent shapes
450g (1lb) canned lychees, drained
225g (8oz) canned pineapple chunks, drained (or pieces of fresh pineapple)
2 fresh mangoes, peeled and sliced
Few seedless grapes, white and black, halved
1 small melon, cut into chunks
¼ water-melon, cut into chunks
4 fresh figs, halved

Dressing
30ml (2 tblsp) lemon juice
Pinch salt
50g (2oz) chopped toasted walnut or pine kernels

Prepare the fruits as suggested and arrange in a large glass bowl, in layers. Spoon over the lemon juice and sprinkle with salt. Sprinkle over the chopped nuts.

Facing page: Frozen Lemon Yogurt Soufflé (top left), Tropical Fruit Dessert (top right) and Tropical Fruit Salad (bottom).

Passion Fruit Ice Cream

PREPARATION TIME: 20 minutes plus freezing time

SERVES: 4 people

6 passion fruit
300ml (½ pint) thick natural yogurt
2 egg yolks
10ml (2 tsp) honey

To Decorate
1-2 passion fruit, halved and scooped

For the ice cream: halve the passion fruit and scoop all the centre pulp into a bowl. Add the

This page: Banana, Orange and Almond Truffles (top) and Hazelnut and Apple Meringue Torten (bottom). Facing page: Passion Fruit Ice Cream (top) and Strawberry and Melon Salad (bottom).

yogurt, egg yolks and honey, and mix well together. Pour into a shallow container and freeze until firm. Scoop the ice cream into stemmed glasses and trickle a little passion fruit pulp over each portion. Serve immediately.
Note: this ice cream goes *very* hard and needs to be removed from the freezer several minutes before scooping.

Suji Halwa
(SEMOLINA PUDDING)

PREPARATION TIME: 5-6 minutes

COOKING TIME: 10 minutes

100-125g (4-5oz) coarse semolina
75-100g (3-4oz) unsalted or
    clarified butter
25-50g (1-2oz) mixed almond and
    cashew nuts
25-50g (1-2oz) raisins or sultanas
75-100g (3-4oz) sugar
250-300ml (8-10 fl oz) water
8 small cardamoms, seeds removed
    and ground

It is important to use a large enough saucepan as semolina will increase to twice its volume. Dry roast semolina in a non-stick pan for 2-3 minutes, until it turns light brown. Remove to a dish. Melt butter or clarified butter and add nuts and raisins. Fry for 1 minute, then add semolina. Add sugar and water. Sprinkle with ground cardamom seeds. Cover and cook on a low heat for 3-4 minutes. Mix well and stir fry for 1-2 minutes until dry. Serve hot or cold.

Ricotta Pancakes with Honey and Raisin Sauce

PREPARATION TIME: 10 minutes

COOKING TIME: 2-3 minutes

SERVES: 4 people

**Facing page: Sevian Ki
Kheer (top) and Suji Halwa
(bottom). Ricotta Pancakes
with Honey and Raisin
Sauce (above) and Almond
Stuffed Figs (left).**

Sauce
60ml (4 tblsp) clear honey
Juice ½ lemon
15ml (1 tblsp) raisins
15ml (1 tblsp) pine kernels

Filling
225g (8oz) curd cheese, or Ricotta
Grated rind of ½ lemon
30ml (2 tblsp) raisins
15ml (1 tblsp) chopped pine kernels

8 small, hot pancakes

To Decorate
Twists of lemon

For the sauce: put all the ingredients into a small pan and warm through gently. For the filling: beat the cheese and the lemon rind until soft; mix in the raisins and pine kernels. Divide the filling amongst the hot pancakes and either roll them up, or fold them into triangles. Arrange the pancakes on warm plates, spoon the sauce over the top and decorate with twists of lemon. Serve immediately.

Glazed Cherry Rice Pudding

PREPARATION TIME: 20 minutes, plus cooling and chilling time

COOKING TIME: 45 minutes to 1 hour

SERVES: 4-6 people

60g (2oz) brown rice
25g (1oz) soft brown sugar
600ml (1 pint) skimmed milk
2.5ml (½ tsp) vanilla essence
Generous pinch ground nutmeg
30ml (2 tblsp) thick natural yogurt
225g (8oz) fresh cherries, de-stalked and pitted
150ml (¼ pint) pure red grape juice
150ml (¼ pint) water
10ml (2 tsp) agar agar

Put the rice, sugar, skimmed milk, vanilla essence and nutmeg into a solid based pan; bring to the boil and simmer gently for ¾-1 hour,

until the rice mixture is thick and creamy. Allow to cool and then beat in the yogurt. Spoon into a glass bowl and arrange the cherries on the top. Mix the grape juice with half the water; dissolve the agar agar in the remaining water and then add to the grape juice. Leave in a cool place until syrupy. Spoon the red glaze evenly over the cherries. Chill until set.

Iced Kiwi Fruit and Yogurt Pudding

PREPARATION TIME: 15 minutes, plus chilling time

SERVES: 4 people

300ml (½ pint) thick natural yogurt
Artificial sweetener to taste, or a little honey
4 kiwi fruit, peeled and chopped

2 kiwi fruit, peeled and thinly sliced

Mix the yogurt with sweetener or honey to taste, and stir in the chopped kiwi fruit. Place slices of kiwi fruit so that they stand upright against the sides of 4 stemmed glasses; spoon the yogurt and kiwi fruit mixture into the centre. Chill briefly, for about 20-30 minutes, before serving.

Strawberry and Melon Salad

PREPARATION TIME: 25 minutes

SERVES: 4 people

225g (8oz) large strawberries, hulled
1 small Charentais or Ogen melon
Juice of 1 orange
15ml (1 tblsp) brandy

To Decorate
Small sprigs fresh mint

Facing page: Glazed Cherry Rice Pudding (left) and Iced Kiwi Fruit and Yogurt Pudding (right).

Slice the strawberries quite thinly. Halve and de-seed the melon and then scoop it into small balls (there is a special cutter for doing this, but you can do it with a coffee spoon). Arrange the strawberry slices and melon balls on individual glass plates. Mix the orange juice with the brandy and dribble over the fruit. Decorate with mint.

Banana, Almond and Orange Truffles

PREPARATION TIME: 25 minutes

MAKES: 10

2 bananas, peeled
Juice of ½ orange
Finely grated rind of 1 orange
100g (4oz) ground almonds
30ml (2 tblsp) finely chopped
   blanched almonds
15ml (1 tblsp) dark, soft brown sugar
Plain chocolate vermicelli

Mash the bananas with the orange juice and rind; mix in the ground almonds, chopped almonds and brown sugar. Chill the mixture until it is firm enough to shape. Roll into small balls, about the size of a ping pong ball. Roll each one in chocolate vermicelli so as to give an even coating. Chill once again.

Grapefruit Shrub

PREPARATION TIME: 10-15
                     minutes

SERVES: 4 people

Peeled segments from 2 grapefruit
300ml (½ pint) unsweetened
   grapefruit juice
150ml (¼ pint) water
30ml (2 tblsp) clear honey
2 egg whites

To Decorate
Small sprigs fresh mint or grated
   lemon rind

Put the grapefruit segments, grapefruit juice, water and honey into the liquidiser and blend until smooth. Add the egg whites and blend once again until frothy. Pour into glasses, making sure that a good portion of the white 'froth' goes into each one. Decorate with mint or lemon rind.

Sevian Ki Kheer

PREPARATION TIME: 5 minutes

COOKING TIME: 15 minutes

25g (1oz) unsalted butter
1 bayleaf
100g (4oz) fine vermicelli
600ml (1 pint) milk reduced to
   450 ml (¾) pint
50-75g (2-3oz) sugar
8 small cardamoms, seeds removed
   and ground
25g (1oz) raisins
25g (1oz) almonds, chopped

Melt butter in a pan and fry bayleaf for 1-2 minutes. Add broken vermicelli and fry for 1 minute. Add milk, sugar and ground cardamom seeds. Gently simmer for 5-6 minutes. Add raisins. Gently stir pudding once or twice during cooking to stop it burning. Remove from heat, pour into a serving dish, sprinkle with chopped almonds. Serve hot or cold.

Tropical Fruit Flummery

PREPARATION TIME: 10 minutes

SERVES: 4 people

3 kiwi fruit, peeled and chopped
2 ripe nectarines, halved, stoned and
   chopped
2 slices fresh pineapple, peeled and
   chopped
Juice of 1 fresh lime
300ml (½ pint) unsweetened
   pineapple juice

To Decorate
Slices of peeled kiwi fruit, or lime

Put the kiwi fruit, nectarines, pineapple, lime juice and pineapple juice into the liquidiser and blend until smooth. Pour into tall glasses and top up with iced water (either mineral or tap water). Decorate the rim of each glass with a slice of kiwi fruit or lime.

Almond Stuffed Figs

PREPARATION TIME: 25 minutes

SERVES: 4 people

4 large ripe figs
60ml (4 tblsp) ground almonds
30ml (2 tblsp) orange juice
30ml (2 tblsp) finely chopped dried
   apricots

Sauce
60ml (4 tblsp) natural yogurt
Finely grated rind of ½ orange

Garnish
Wedges of ripe fig
Wedges of lime
Ground cinnamon

Make a cross cut in each fig, without cutting right down and through the base. Ease the four sections of each fig out, rather like a flower head. Mix the ground allmonds with the orange juice and chopped dried apricots; press into the centre of each fig. For the sauce: mix the yogurt with the orange rind, and thin down with *a little* water. Spoon a pool of orange flavoured yogurt onto each of 4 small plates; sit a stuffed fig in the centre of each one. Decorate with wedges of fig and lime and a sprinkling of ground cinnamon.

Hazelnut and Apple Meringue Torten

PREPARATION TIME: 25-30
                     minutes

COOKING TIME: 45 minutes

OVEN: 190°C, 375°F, Gas Mark 5,
then 160°C, 325°F, Gas Mark 3

SERVES: 6-8 people

100g (4oz) butter
50g (2oz) soft brown sugar
100g (4oz) wholemeal flour
50g (2oz) ground hazelnuts
30ml (2 tblsp) chopped hazelnuts
2 egg whites

75g (3oz) golden granulated sugar
300ml (½ pint) thick unsweetened
  apple puree

Work the butter, brown sugar,
wholemeal flour and ground
hazelnuts to a soft, smooth dough.
Knead lightly and work in the

**This page: Tropical Fruit
Flummery (left) and
Grapefruit Shrub (right).**

chopped hazelnuts. Press evenly
over the base of a 23cm (9 inch)
fluted, loose-bottomed flan tin.

Bake in the oven for 10 minutes. Meanwhile, whisk the egg whites until stiff but not 'dry'; gradually whisk in the golden granulated sugar. Remove the shortcake from the oven and pipe or swirl the meringue in a border around the edge. Return to the oven, lower the heat, and bake for a further 35 minutes, until golden. Fill immediately with the apple puree and serve while still warm.

Blackcurrant Sherbet

PREPARATION TIME: 10 minutes

100-175g or 4-6oz fresh or frozen
    blackcurrants
750ml (1¼ pints) water
50-60g or 2-3oz sugar
Pinch of salt
15ml (1 tblsp) lemon juice
Ice cubes

Mash blackcurrants in a bowl or blend them in a liquidiser. Add water and mix well, then strain. Dissolve sugar and salt and add lemon juice. Serve with ice cubes.

Spicy Fresh Mango Juice

PREPARATION TIME: 15 minutes

SERVES: 4 people

300ml (½ pint) fresh mango pulp
Juice of 1 lemon
15ml (1 tblsp) clear honey
Generous pinch ground ginger
Generous pinch nutmeg
150ml (¼ pint) unsweetened orange
    juice
150ml (¼ pint) water
1 small piece fresh root ginger

To Decorate
4 rings of orange

Put the mango pulp, lemon juice, honey, ground ginger, nutmeg, orange juice and water into the liquidiser and blend until smooth. Pour into 4 glasses, adding two or three ice cubes to each one. Put the piece of root ginger into a garlic

crusher and squeeze a few drops into each glass. Slide a ring of orange over the rim of each glass and serve.

Mulled Apple and Honey

PREPARATION TIME: 5 minutes

COOKING TIME: 4 minutes

SERVES: 4 people

450ml (¾ pint) unsweetened apple
    juice
150ml (¼ pint) water
10ml (2 tsp) honey
2 cinnamon sticks, split in half
6 cloves
3 strips lemon peel

To Serve
4 cinnamon sticks

Put the apple juice into a pan with the water, honey, broken cinnamon sticks, cloves and lemon peel; simmer very gently for 4 minutes. Remove the broken cinnamon sticks and pour liquid into heat-proof glasses. Spike each drink with a whole cinnamon stick and serve.

Passion Fruit Sherbet

PREPARATION TIME: 10 minutes

8-10 passion fruits
750ml (1¼ pints) water
Sugar
Pinch of salt
1-2 drops of red food colouring
    (optional)
Ice cubes

Cut passion fruits in half. Remove the pulp and blend with the water. Strain and dissolve sugar; add salt. Add red food colouring, if desired, this will make the sherbet pink. Serve with ice cubes.

This page: Blackcurrant Sherbet (centre) and Passion Fruit Sherbet (right). Facing page: Mulled Apple and Honey (left) and Spicy Fresh Mango Juice (right).